MARLBOROUGH

JOHN CHURCHILL, DUKE OF MARLBOROUGH

from a woodcut by Eric King

MARLBOROUGH

by MAURICE ASHLEY

Great Lives

LONDON
GERALD DUCKWORTH & CO. LTD.
NEW YORK
THE MACMILLAN COMPANY

First published   1939
Reprinted 1941, 1947, 1957

First published in the United States in 1956

Printed by Offset litho
in Great Britain by
Phototype Ltd., London

To

PHYLLIS

CONTENTS

CHRONOLOGY

1650. May 26th.	Born.
1667. September 14th.	Commission as Ensign.
1672. March–May.	At sea.
1674.	Fighting under Turenne in Flanders.
1678.	Marriage.
1679–81.	With James, Duke of York, in Brussels and Edinburgh.
1685. July 5th.	Battle of Sedgemoor.
1688. November.	Glorious Revolution. Churchill at Salisbury.
1689.	Marlborough in Flanders under Waldeck.
1690. September.	Campaign in Ireland.
1692. January.	Dismissed from Army.
1696. Summer.	Fenwick case.
1698. April.	Marlborough restored to favour.
1701. August.	Conclusion of Grand Alliance.
1702. February.	Accession of Queen Anne.
1704. July 2nd.	Battle of the Schellenberg.
August 13th.	Battle of Blenheim.
1706. May 23rd.	Battle of Ramillies.
1708. July 11th.	Battle of Oudenarde.

1709.	May.	The Allied "preliminaries."
	September 11th.	Battle of Malplaquet.
1711.	December 31st.	Marlborough dismissed.
1712.	November.	Marlborough leaves England.
1714.	August 1st.	Death of Queen Anne; Marlborough returns.
1722.	June 5th.	Death of Marlborough.

Dates of events in England are given in Old Style, of events in Europe in New Style ; the difference between Old Style and New was ten days in the seventeenth century and eleven days in the eighteenth century.

FOREWORD

DURING the years 1929–34 I had the privilege of acting as research assistant to Mr. Winston Churchill when he was writing the earlier volumes of his great biography of Marlborough. In that capacity I had access to the Blenheim Palace archives and Spencer papers and also paid visits to the official collections in Paris and Vienna. Now that Mr. Churchill's work has been completed, I have taken advantage of the opportunity afforded by this series to epitomize my own views on the first Duke of Marlborough ; these differ in emphasis and on a few specific points from those of Mr. Churchill. However, this " Great Life " is written largely in the hope that it may interest readers sufficiently to induce them to embark upon Mr. Churchill's four remarkable volumes, in which they will find not only a complete apologia for the Duke but the materials on which to form their own independent judgment of his character.

M. A.

HENDON,
February, 1939.

CHAPTER I

THE PATH TO FAME: 1650–1688

Birth – education – the Court of Charles II – marriage – James's
servant – battle of Sedgemoor – the Glorious Revolution.

JOHN CHURCHILL, first Duke of Marlborough,
was the ablest soldier who ever commanded the
British Army and the most talented general who
ever served the British Crown. He was the
least jealous and best beloved of commanders-in-
chief. The strongest rebuke said to have been
administered by him was a message through his
secretary, " my Lord Duke is surprised." He
never chided a servant or spoke harshly to an
N.C.O. The soul of charm, grace and courtesy,
there were few who knew him intimately who
did not yield to his spell. Yet there was dross
among the gold. A first-rate soldier, he was a
second-rate statesman. As a politician he was
in the main simply an ambitious opportunist
who could not bear to be out of office. Excel-
ling chiefly in those diplomatic manœuvres
which would advance himself or his army, he
seldom, if ever, exerted his influence for the
causes of peace or justice in which he was not
directly concerned. His avarice and meanness made him a laughing-stock. He clung
zealously to the trappings and emoluments that
went with military power, even writing on
occasion abject letters to his political opponents
so as to ensure that he should in no

circumstances lose his estates. In Lord Morley's phrase, he was an instance of that " strange dualism in men which makes them . . . sometimes strong and sometimes weak."

John Churchill was born at Ash House near the village of Musbury in Devonshire in the early hours of May 26, 1650. He barely survived the dangers of seventeenth-century childbirth. Out of twelve brothers and sisters only five lived beyond childhood. John himself was born a weakling and not expected to live, as is shown by his immediate baptism at Ash House on the day of his birth. His father, Winston Churchill, was a small landowner who fought on the Cavalier side in the Civil War. Twice fined for his royalism, he reared his family in decent obscurity during the Cromwellian era. But John Churchill's mother (a Drake distantly connected with Sir Francis' family) came of a Roundhead family and it was in the security of his maternal grandmother's house that he was born.

The education which Winston Churchill provided for his eldest surviving son was brief but varied and useful. Winston himself instilled those principles of veneration for the institution of monarchy and the Protestant religion which his son never entirely forgot. Soon after the Restoration of King Charles II Winston was given a small appointment at Dublin. Thus John went for a time to the Dublin City Free School, but was afterwards transferred to St. Paul's School in the City of London. He learned

to write and spell well enough for practical
purposes and acquired a smattering of Latin.
But his wider education was to be obtained in
service at the Court of Charles II, where he
picked up French, dabbled in astronomy, saw
the plays of Shakespeare and acquired all the
graces of society life.

Meanwhile, his sister Arabella, who was two
years his senior, had been making steady worldly
progress. A plainish girl with nice legs, she had
caught the roving eye of the King's only brother,
James, Duke of York, afterwards King James II,
and she combined the duties of Maid of Honour
to the first Duchess of York with those of mistress to the Duchess' husband. To her, clearly,
John owed his appointment as page to James,
Duke of York, which he obtained at about the
age of sixteen, although Winston (now knighted)
held the view that " it is no great preferment
to be a page." However, there was the adoles-
cent John Churchill, handsome, well-mannered,
with an influential sister, ensconced in the
highest circles of English society, and he used
all his opportunities.

Three very different women played their
parts in the life of John Churchill. First, Arabella. Then his distant kinswoman, the exotic
Barbara Villiers, Duchess of Cleveland, first
mistress en titre to King Charles II, whose lover
Churchill was to become. Finally Sarah Jennings, a haughty and respectable but lovely
Maid of Honour, who was to be Churchill's
wife. For ten years, from the age of seventeen
to twenty-seven, he mixed his sexual and military

experiences in well-chosen proportions. In September, 1667, he secured a commission as ensign and served at Tangier, then an English possession, and also aboard the Fleet against the Mediterranean pirates. On his return to England, this graceful, engaging ensign with fair hair and blue eyes, now twenty-two years old, became the father to one of the Duchess of Cleveland's many offspring. By that time Charles II had tired of the lady and when he caught Churchill in her room he said – at least so Court scandal had it – " Go ! You are a rascal, but I forgive you because you do it to get your bread." Barbara was generous to her lovers and, with that monetary carefulness which Churchill was always to show, he invested £4,500 of the money that she bestowed on him in a form of life insurance.

Another interlude of soldiering now occurred. England was engaged in her third war against her trade and naval rivals, the Dutch, and Churchill's First Company of the Guards was aboard the Fleet when it took part in the drawn naval battle of Sole Bay. For his share in the fighting, his patron, James, Duke of York, had him made a captain. In the following year (1673) Captain Churchill went as a volunteer with the Duke of Monmouth, Charles's favourite bastard, to the siege of the Dutch fortress of Maastricht, where he was wounded, saved Monmouth's life, met Louis XIV, the King of France, and generally distinguished himself. So considerable a mark did he make that, although England now withdrew from the war, he was summoned to Paris and appointed colonel in command of one of the English infantry regiments in French pay against the Dutch and their allies of the Holy Roman Empire, and fought under the famous French general, Turenne. The English Government was informed towards the end of the campaign that " no one in the world could possibly have done better than Mr. Churchill has done and M. de Turenne is very well pleased with all our nation."

On his return to Court, Churchill's amours became so notorious that they seemed likely to submerge his newly acquired military reputation. The reports of the French Ambassador in England which reached Versailles in November, 1676, told of how he had left Barbara Cleveland " after pillaging her of 100,000 livres " and was seeking marriage with the pretty but quarrelsome sixteen-year-old Sarah Jennings. In spite of Turenne's tribute and Louis XIV's direct knowledge, the story was circulated that he was winning his way exclusively through feminine influence, and the French War Minister said nastily that his master did not want " dishonourable and dishonoured carpet knights in his armies." But John Churchill was indifferent now to offers of regiments. He fell in love as most men fall in love once only in their lives. If he did not at first seek marriage – as some of Sarah's notes to him suggest – he was soon impelled to do so. The girl's off-handedness and harsh treatment of her suitor and his parents' opposition heightened his desire. Somewhere and at some time about 1678 (exactly where or when is not known)

BM

Captain John Churchill and Sarah Jennings
were married. The " good fairy " at their
marriage, in Mr. Churchill's words, was Sarah's
mistress, Mary of Modena, second wife of James,
Duke of York. Ten years later – such are the
exigencies of political life – we shall see John and
Sarah egging on Mary of Modena's step-daughter
to blackguard the character and morals of this
" good fairy " of their wedding day.

The married life of the Churchills opened in
what was for persons of their class and ambitions a condition of comparative poverty. John
had to manage on the rather variable perquisites of a Colonel of Foot, a commission
which he was allowed to purchase in February,
1678, and on his salary as Gentleman of the
Bedchamber and later Master of the Wardrobe
to James, Duke of York. To maintain their
place in high society without private means
demanded the most rigid economy. At first the
ambitious young couple could afford no home of
their own and Sarah was packed off to live with
her parents-in-law in the country. Sarah
promptly quarrelled with her mother-in-law, as
she had previously quarrelled with her own
mother, and ultimately John took a house in
Jermyn Street, London, where he had had his
bachelor lodgings.

There is no doubt that it was in these years
of scraping and straitened circumstances that
Churchill acquired those habits of " meanness "
and " avarice " for which he was famous throughout his life. The need to earn an adequate

income bound him to his master, the increasingly unpopular Duke of York. At first he had hopes of an active army career at a time when Charles II's foreign policy required France to be threatened with an Anglo-Dutch alliance. Churchill was sent over to concert arrangements with the Dutch prince, William of Orange, who had just married James's elder daughter, Mary. But the French and Dutch made peace, and for the next five years, at the height of James's unpopularity, Churchill had to act as glorified messenger boy and valet to one of the most hated men in England.

It had been known for some years that the heir-presumptive to the English throne was an enthusiastic Roman Catholic, and his brother Charles II's efforts to decree toleration for members of that Church had roused the fears and jealousies of the Anglican Parliament. In 1678 a shady informer named Titus Oates had come forward with the story of a Popish plot which shook England from top to bottom. The House of Commons tried to secure the enactment of an Exclusion Bill which would have prevented the Catholic James from succeeding to the throne, and Charles, though determined by hook or crook to save James's hereditary rights, thought it best that he should leave the country. In March, 1679, Churchill had therefore to accompany him to his exile in Brussels.

During the years of exile Churchill made himself indispensable to James, but at the same time was clever enough neither to offend his master's opponents nor to cause his master to

suspect his own loyalty. His earliest biographer
states that Churchill was against Exclusion " and
told me he thought it the highest act of injus-
tice for anyone to be set aside from his inheritance upon bare suppositions of intended evils."
Those who opposed Exclusion came to be known
as Tories and thus for the next twenty-five
years Churchill ranked as a leading Tory. He
went on missions to Charles II and to Louis
XIV, asking them to exert their influence on
James's behalf, but he also allowed himself to
be pressed by his friends at Court to keep James
away from Whitehall. In 1680 and 1681
James's place of exile was shifted from Brussels
to Edinburgh, where he was appointed Royal
Commissioner and behaved with harshness and
stupidity. Churchill was careful to let it be known
that he did not approve of this conduct or of
any idea of James acting independently of Whitehall, and even went so far as to write to a friend
at Court, after a vain attempt had been made
to reconvert James to Protestantism, that, without this, " sooner or later we must be all undone."
But, by tact or dissimulation, he retained the
Duke's confidence, and when in 1682 Charles
finally outmanœuvred the Exclusionists or Whigs,
as they were now called, James could return
to London and Churchill could claim his rewards,
a barony in the peerage of Scotland and the
combined emoluments of two regiments.

For the last three years of King Charles II's
reign no Parliament met, no war came and
James virtually governed the country. This
was a period of profit and ease for the new

Lord Churchill, who basked in favour at Court.
Dr. Gilbert Burnet, afterwards Bishop of Salisbury, who was later to know the two Churchills
intimately, wrote of him about this time:

He knew the arts of living in a Court beyond
any man in it. He caressed all people with a
soft and obliging deportment, and was always
ready to do good offices. He had no fortune
to set up on : this put him on all the methods
of acquiring one. And that went so far into
him, that he did not shake it off when he was
in a much higher elevation : nor was his expense suited enough to his posts.

In 1683 a new accession of money, office and
influence came to the Churchill fortunes. His
wife sought and obtained an appointment as
Lady of the Bedchamber to Princess Anne,
James's second daughter, when her marriage to
Prince George of Denmark required her to set
up a separate establishment, and later Sarah
was promoted First Lady, with her salary doubled.
Anne, like all the Stuarts, was passionately
attached to favourites. She once wrote to Sarah
warning her against another woman and remind-
ing her of " what the song says – to be jealous is
the fault of every tender lover." Sarah retained
Anne's affection for about twenty years, while
Churchill came to share her valuable favour.
During this period the Churchills enjoyed the
blessing of healthy children, although their first
child had died in infancy. John was always a
devoted paterfamilias who delighted in sunning
himself in his family mansions. But from domestic

joys and sinecure duties he was compelled to
turn when in February, 1685, the opportunist
Charles II died and a Roman Catholic king
ruled a Protestant realm.

As during the last seven years of Charles's
reign, Churchill continued to be a foremost and
trusted servant of King James II and to acquire
offices and honours, which included an English
peerage and the Governorship of the Hudson's
Bay Company ; but at the same time he tactfully expressed his disagreement with the King's
policy. James's intention was to stretch his pre-
rogatives to the utmost to acquire equality, if
not predominance, for his fellow religionists and
to attain a position not dissimilar from that of
the neighbouring autocrat, Louis XIV of France.
But at first he half-hid his intentions. When he
sent Lord Churchill to inform Louis of his accession to the Throne, he cancelled his original
orders ·to ask for a subsidy such as Louis had
been accustomed to dole out to Charles II. At
the outset of his reign James had a loyal Parliament and he promised to respect the rights
of the Church of England.

Thus it was that when James's half-brother,
the Duke of Monmouth, invaded England in
the Protestant cause in June, 1685, he chose a
most unpropitious moment and few wealthy or
influential men joined him. This western invasion afforded Churchill an opportunity for an
independent display of his military gifts. In
spite of his meagre experience, he was entrusted
by James with the command of the troops sent

to repel Monmouth's brave but poorly-armed
volunteer force in Somerset. Once Churchill
came into contact with Monmouth, though with
only a small body of cavalry, he never let go.
He clung on to him, cutting off the stragglers,
until Monmouth ventured on the desperate but
not ill-considered course of a night attack on
the Royal Army as it lay encamped on the field
of Sedgemoor (July 5). As soon as Churchill
heard of the surprise, he came hastily on the
scene, reinforced the Royalist flank where it
was weakest, and at dawn organized a successful
attack which captured the enemy's artillery. To
him was due the main credit for the victory, but
before the battle he had been superseded in the
nominal command by a naturalized Frenchman,
Lord Feversham. Churchill was resentful. This
personal factor further alienated him from
James II.

The easy suppression of the rebellion en-
couraged the obstinate James on the most
autocratic courses. But he first had the rebels
viciously punished, to the open displeasure of
Churchill. James used the rebellion as an
excuse to build a large standing army, which
he filled with Roman Catholic officers and
encamped on Hounslow Heath to overawe
London. He introduced a new ecclesiastical
court to act as a curb on the Church of England.
He forced Roman Catholics into office everywhere, even into positions from which they had
been specifically excluded by Act of Parliament.
A secret Protestant opposition was gradually
created in which Whigs joined with Tories and

entered into treasonable correspondence with
James's son-in-law, William of Orange. Churchill,
a sincere Protestant, resisted the pressure brought
upon all Court dignitaries to enter the Roman
Catholic Church and seems to have told James
that he disapproved of what he was doing. But
he did not resign his offices and instead successfully used his wife's and his own growing influence with James's fervently Anglican daughter
Anne to carry her over to the opposition camp.
Churchill himself assured William that he was
resolved, "although I cannot live the life of a
saint, if there ever be occasion for it, to show
the resolution of a martyr." In the summer of
1688 an unexpected blow fell upon this secret
opposition : Mary of Modena bore James a male
heir. Hitherto the hope had prevailed that
James's early death and the accession of the
Protestant Mary of Orange would put a speedy
end to the Catholicizing policy ; now its indefinite continuance was promised. Sarah, Anne
and the rest hastened to spread the false story
that the birth was an imposture, and under the
Churchills' influence Anne wrote a series of
nauseating letters to her sister to that effect.
The conspirators then invited William to cross
the sea and save England and her Church from
James and his infant. Churchill, a little later,
wrote independently, putting his honour in
William's hands and again asserting that he was
ready to die for his religion.

In November William landed in Tor Bay with
a large army and Churchill prepared to go over
to him. He first arranged for Sarah and Anne

to join William at an appropriate moment, while his brother George, who was in the Navy, was to help carry over the Fleet. His own job was to neutralize and, if possible, enlist the Army in the cause of revolution. James, betrayed on all sides, still trusted this man who had been his page and servant and appointed him lieutenant-general, taking him to Salisbury to confront William's motley Protestant horde. Churchill first tried to kidnap the king and take him to William. This move, which might have prevented war, is vouched for not only by contemporary Royalist authorities but also by the French Ambassador who was with James and Churchill at Salisbury. Churchill must have realized that if it came to a clash between James at the head of the English Army and a foreign army officered by Dutchmen – who had been England's enemies for a generation – the rebellion would be defeated. There was a significant pointer to the Army's attitude when another traitor officer, Lord Cornbury, tried to lead some troops across the lines and they refused to follow him. It is all the more surprising therefore that at this critical moment, at a council of war, Churchill should have urged James to fight. This advice – which could only have been given because Churchill knew that it would not be followed – was the very depth of double dealing. But James refused to advance and thereby sealed his fate. Princess Anne joined William safely and, thanks in part to the plotting of the Churchills, a bloodless revolution was effected.

Churchill's part in the revolution was deliberately

unscrupulous. As a Protestant he disliked James's measures ; as a man of unsatisfied ambitions he had his grievances. But he would not burn his boats until he must. It was against his nature to resign his commissions or to commit himself irretrievably by joining the exiles in Holland, for then he could not have righted himself with the King if things went wrong. He did make an attempt to compromise between personal interest and abhorrence of James's policy by seeking command of an English regiment abroad, but what he would never do was to exclude himself from the thick of events.

CHAPTER II

REWARDS AND PUNISHMENTS : 1689–1702

Command in Flanders and Ireland – opposition to William III –
   the Fenwick affair – reconciliation and promotion – the
   Grand Alliance.

CHURCHILL tactfully refrained from voting for
the establishment of a regency when the throne
was declared " vacant," and this Tory project,
to which William was adamantly opposed, was
defeated by two votes in the House of Lords.
The Churchills' influence was exerted to persuade Anne to waive her hereditary right to
the immediate succession in order that William
might remain King even should his wife, Anne's
elder sister, predecease him. Churchill was re-
warded by being created an earl with the title of
Marlborough, by being made a member of the
Privy Council and one of the nine Lord Justices
who governed England in William's absence, and
by being confirmed in his lieutenant-generalship.
But he did not regard these honours as sufficient ;
he hankered after the lucrative post of Master-
General of the Ordnance and a supreme command. He resented the fact that William gave
the command of his army in Flanders to a man
of sixty-nine and of his army in Ireland to one
of eighty. The truth was that, largely because
of Marlborough's power over Princess Anne, the
new monarchs never had full confidence in him ;
William thought him " very assuming " and

Mary told her husband : " I can never either
trust or esteem him." In due course Marlborough
was to reciprocate by stirring up opposition to
William in the Army. But first he showed his
military worth in Flanders and Ireland.

William had come to England, not out of any
altruistic regard for English liberties, but to make
certain of her participation in the coming war
against Louis XIV. He laboured to build a
Grand Alliance against the French King, who
had declared war on Holland as the Dutch ruler
was on his way to England. Thus, immediately
after the Revolution of 1688, England and
Holland went to war with France. In the summer
of 1689 Marlborough distinguished himself at
the Battle of Walcourt in Flanders, where he
headed the Household Cavalry in a counter-
attack on the French. Meanwhile, James II,
with French and Irish troops, had been defeated
at the Battle of the Boyne in Ireland, and Marlborough, on his own initiative, volunteered to
cap this success by capturing the towns of Cork
and Kinsale in the six weeks which remained of
the campaigning season of 1690. Co-operating
closely with the Fleet, he accomplished in twenty-
three days what William's Dutch commanders
had failed to do in a year. But he was found no
further independent employment and his indigna-
tion knew no bounds. Overpowering and unscrupulous ambition henceforward guided his conduct. When in the next year William offered
to take him to Flanders as Lieutenant-General,
Marlborough refused to go except as commander
of the English troops, and preferred to stay in

London to raise opposition and foment discontent
against the monarch whom he had helped to
establish on the Throne.

Marlborough's campaign against William –
the least successful of his campaigns – was based
on a mixed crew of allies. First he took steps
to secure his line of retreat by opening a correspondence with the Court of St. Germains in
France, to which the defeated and betrayed
James II had now retired. He induced Princess
Anne to write a contrite letter to the father she
had abandoned. James himself seems to have
been fool enough to believe Marlborough's
message of penitence and to credit his promises
of help. William had speedily made himself so
unpopular with his English subjects that the
possibility of a Jacobite restoration, especially if
he were defeated in the French war, was serious.
So Marlborough was not the only eminent
Englishman to enter into these intrigues to safeguard himself. But in Princess Anne there was
another and a Protestant candidate for the rever-
sion of the throne. Marlborough won her gratitude
by compelling William to raise her allowance
from £30,000 to £50,000, and his wife encour-
aged her to speak of William as " Mr. Caliban "
and the " Dutch abortion." It was no wonder
that a personal quarrel broke out between Mary
and her sister over Sarah's position and influence.
William was warned that Marlborough's parliamentary attacks and Army cabals were a move
in the interests of Anne. With these impulses
to action William hit back swiftly, and Marlborough was dismissed from all his offices, while

Mary, less wisely, had him thrown into the Tower
on what proved to be a false charge of con-
spiracy.

On his release on bail in 1692, Marlborough
redoubled his intrigues against William and
entered into a closer correspondence with St.
Germains.   In the House of Lords he was the
most enthusiastic exponent of an amendment to
a new Treason Bill to the effect that an English
peer must henceforward be tried by the entire
House of Lords, even if Parliament were not
sitting, instead of, as previously, by a special
commission chosen by the King. William was,
of course, reluctant to facilitate the defence of
peers at a time when treason was rife. That
Marlborough was guilty of treason there was no
doubt. He sent a number of encouraging messages to James II and, although the famous
letter which Macaulay and other historians
supposed him to have written betraying an
English naval attack on Brest in 1694 is in all
probability a forgery, it may be that he made
some casual remark to one of the Jacobite emis-
saries in England after he had ascertained that
this information had already reached Louis XIV
from other sources.   His cold wrath against
William could easily have overcome his loyalty
to that extent. He certainly did not betray to
the exiled King any naval or military information of value, if only for the simple reason that,
being out of office, he had no secrets to betray.
Nor was this kind of treason what William suspected.   William knew, and did not care, that
not only Marlborough, but some of his Ministers

to safeguard their skins and estates were at this
time writing friendly letters to St. Germains.
William's real grudge against Marlborough was
that he was trying to turn the English Parliament
and English Army against the Crown when in
the midst of the war with France.

At the end of 1694 Queen Mary died childless
and Princess Anne was brought a step nearer
the succession. Marlborough now felt it to be
in his own interest to patch up his differences
with William. He made an indirect offer of his
services, and when William achieved his one
personal success of the war, he induced Princess
Anne to write a congratulatory letter to the King.
William gradually responded to these overtures.
In the following year, when a certain Jacobite,
Sir John Fenwick, was arrested for plotting a
rising in England and in his confession charged
Marlborough among others with a treasonable
correspondence with King James, William took
not the slightest notice. Marlborough, in evident
confidence that Fenwick had no letters of his to
back the accusations, put a bold face on the
business. He pressed on an Act of Attainder to
ensure Fenwick's conviction, while his brother
George exclaimed, " Thrust a bullet down his
throat. Dead men tell no tales ! " But at the
same time Marlborough took the precaution of
frightening out of the country Lord Ailesbury,
another Jacobite who had been on that side of
the divided Jacobite camp with which he had in
fact been in communication. And therefore,
when the French war was over, but not before,

William could restore Marlborough's offices and as a further mark of reconciliation appoint him governor to Anne's nine-year-old son, the Duke of Gloucester.

The Treaty of Ryswick (1697), by which the long conflict between William III and Louis XIV was brought to an end, was a compromise. For nine years Louis had fought against England, Holland, Spain, Savoy, Austria and many German princes and had held his own. In the Treaty he kept the conquests won in earlier wars and gained the important town of Strasbourg, although he surrendered in exchange three German towns which he had taken. To secure their frontier, the Dutch were permitted to maintain garrisons in the Spanish Netherlands (Belgium) and William was recognized as King of England. But the Treaty did not look like a permanent settlement, for it was known that one reason which induced Louis to sign an instrument which left him in a weaker position than when Charles II ruled England was the approaching extinction of the Spanish Habsburg line. With the death of Charles the Sufferer, the last Spanish Habsburg, the break-up of the vast Spanish Empire seemed certain. Louis, whose wife was the half-sister of Charles the Sufferer, hoped to profit extensively and was anxious to concentrate his superb diplomatic resources on preparing for the delightful eventuality.

William was, of course, well aware of all this and knew that the possession of Spanish Flanders by the French Crown would be the greatest menace imaginable to the strategic security of

England and Holland. He set himself to prevent
the danger. He had reason to know that,
although he was of the same age as Marlborough,
he had not much longer to live. If his life's
work of preserving the Dutch Republic against
the ambitions of France was to be continued, he
had to find a successor who would maintain the
Anglo-Dutch alliance. After toying with the
idea of remarriage, he chose instead to adopt a
chance which would take into full account the
feelings of the English ruling classes. Princess
Anne, the Protestant heir to the Throne, who had
an apparently healthy son in the Duke of
Gloucester, was a popular figure. Her friend
and adviser, Marlborough, was the best English
general. Whilst his intrigues were but the spite
born of thwarted ambition, his military genius
was enduring. His wife's intimacy with Anne
also made it certain that on William's death he
would be promoted to the highest offices in the
State. Moreover, Marlborough was classed as a
Tory and, with the ending of the war and after
the General Election of 1698, the Tories formed
the majority in the House of Commons. Therefore, for calculable political reasons King William
chose Marlborough as his successor in the struggle
against France.

Marlborough, for his part, was careful to
neglect none of his contacts ; he kept up an
increasingly perfunctory correspondence with
the exiled Jacobites ; he supported the Tory Party
on all party questions ; and he again drew a
draft on Princess Anne's gratitude by pushing

CM

her husband's claim to a large sum of money which William had been reluctant to concede to him. Nevertheless, he welcomed the King's favour.

The half-lunatic King of Spain slowly passed away (November, 1700), but before he did so he bequeathed his throne to Philip of Anjou, grandson of Louis XIV, in order to preserve the unity of his Empire. Although Louis had entered into negotiations with William to divide the Spanish possessions with the Habsburg Austrian Emperor, and had signed two Partition Treaties to this effect, he could not resist this glorious opportunity of family aggrandizement and decided to accept the will. William was shocked to the core : " I am perfectly persuaded," he said, " that if this will be executed England and the Dutch Republic are in the utmost danger of being totally lost and ruined." He therefore urged the Dutch " to oppose so great an evil," and promised " to engage people here, by prudent conduct, by degrees and without perceiving it." Both England and Holland at first recognized the will, so reluctant were they to embark on another war. But Louis XIV's immediate expulsion of the Dutch garrisons from Belgium and his replacing of them by French troops powerfully affected public opinion in both countries. By the middle of 1701 the Opposition parties in London and Amsterdam were begging William to prepare for war. At this crisis William turned to Marlborough ; he appointed him Commander-in-Chief of the English forces and

Ambassador Extraordinary with the task of framing another Grand Alliance to compel the French King to withdraw his troops from Belgium, of preventing the union of France and Spain and of obtaining satisfaction for the Austrian Emperor's claims on the Spanish inheritance.

In his negotiations for the Grand Alliance of 1701, Marlborough disclosed his strength as a diplomatist. He was careful not to offend the constitutional susceptibilities of the English Parliament; he helped to reconcile the sharply opposed claims of the Dutch and the Imperialists; and he saw that the English demands for colonial and trade compensations were met. The terms of the second Grand Alliance were :

(1) That there should be no union between the Crowns of France and Spain ;

(2) that the Austrian Emperor Leopold's second son, the Archduke Charles, should be awarded the Spanish possessions in Belgium and Italy ;

(3) that the Dutch should have a string of fortresses in Belgium to protect them permanently from France ; and

(4) that England and Holland should keep their overseas conquests.

The treaty was signed on September 7, 1701 ; on September 16 James II died and Louis unwisely recognized his son James Edward, known to history as the Old Pretender, as the rightful King of England. This insult rallied the country to the new war. William hastily dissolved Parliament and secured a Whig victory, and the Whigs were rabid for a grand-scale attack on the French. William also had taken the clever precaution of associating Marlborough, the " Tory general," with him in the signature of the Treaty. He had acted just in time. For in February, 1702, he died. Scarcely concealing their pleasure, the Marlboroughs and Anne entered upon their heritage of joy and trouble.

CHAPTER III

Queen Anne and her first Cabinet – War of the Spanish Succession – campaigns of 1702 and 1703 – " No peace without Spain " – obstructions of Dutch and High Tories.

HISTORIANS have recently attempted to revalue the character of Queen Anne, and have even compared her to her predecessor, Queen Elizabeth. But there is some difficulty in fashioning a heroic figure out of this stout, gouty, gluttonous little woman with her dull husband and frequent miscarriages. Her perpetual card-playing, her gambling, her love of tittle-tattle, her schoolgirlish " crushes " and her fancy for drinking spirits out of a teacup – Anne's " cold tea " was a contemporary joke – were harmless habits enough. The essential fact about her was that she was every inch a Stuart, with most of the Stuart faults. She inherited her grandfather Charles I's propensity for Court favourites and also his ingratitude to loyal servants. She possessed all the Stuart obstinacy, but she was lucky in that her obstinacy fitted the mood of the day and her bigotry happened to lie in the direction of the Church of England and not the Church of Rome.

At first all went as William planned. Anne confirmed Marlborough in his post as Commander-in-Chief, awarded him the long-coveted office of Master-General of the Ordnance and

made him in effect her First Minister, the " Grand
Vizier," as an Under-Secretary called him.   He
seized every chance.   War, he knew, was the
sphere of action in which he could employ his
innate genius.   He helped to prepare the Queen's
first speeches in which she promised to carry on
the war against France, and he hurried across
to The Hague to assure the Dutch that, in spite
of the death of their Captain-General, they could
count on the military co-operation of England
and reject any offers of a compromise from
France.   Then Marlborough returned to London
to assist in the construction of Anne's first Cabinet.

The new Government was mainly Tory
in complexion, with an admixture of moderate
Whigs.   Marlborough asked that his conscien-
tious and modest friend, Sidney Godolphin,
should be Lord Treasurer to manage the national
finances and advised that another old friend, the
Whig *magnifico*, the Duke of Shrewsbury, should
be offered a Cabinet post.   Broadly, he and
Queen Anne were agreed that a coalition rather
than a party government was necessary to carry
on the war successfully.   Anne inclined to the
Tories because they were, above all, the Church
of England party, and she was a devoted daughter
of the Church.   Marlborough was then classed
as a Tory, but his views were substantially
modified, not only by the needs of the day but
by the fact that his assertive wife, now promoted
to be Keeper of the Privy Purse, Royal Mistress
of the Robes and Groom of the Stole, was an
outspoken Whig.   Marlborough was not immune
from his wife's effort to make herself a political

figure in the world. There lay a cause of future discord. But meanwhile this somewhat incongruous quartet — Anne, determined, small-minded and hopeful ; Marlborough, at length at the summit of power ; Godolphin, an immaculate but nervous Civil Servant with betting as his moral outlet ; and Sarah, domineering and ambitious — formed the personal basis of the new English Government. Anne wrote in blind affection to Sarah in the following year, " We four must never part till death mows us down with his impartial hand."

War was jointly declared on France by England, Holland and the Emperor on May 15, and a week later Marlborough sailed for the second time to Holland. He was detained for some weeks behind the lines over the troublesome question of who was to succeed William III as Captain-General of the Dutch forces. Marlborough's serene confidence had already made a deep impression at the Hague. Although various princes competed for the honour, the Dutch of their own accord preferred William's implied choice and ultimately Marlborough was appointed to the post at £10,000 a year, which raised his income from his various offices to over £60,000. He concealed his pleasure from the Queen, who had instructed him to procure the post for her stodgy husband, Prince George. Although the post gave Marlborough command over the English and Dutch forces and the numerous mercenaries in their pay, the Dutch Government sent with him on the campaign two deputies whose advice he was bound to seek on questions of high strategy. William had been able to select his own field deputies and consequently had not been hampered by them, but the new deputies had every intention of seeing that the English commander did not jeopardize Dutch security or take undue risks with the Dutch Army.

It thus happened that half the campaigning season was over before Marlborough assumed his command. The French held at the beginning of the war all the fortresses in Belgium, on the Rhine and on the Meuse except Maastricht. They had overrun the territories of the Elector of Cologne and the Bishop of Liége and the Prussian territory of Cleves which adjoined the Dutch Republic. The Dutch, on Marlborough's advice, had laid siege to Kaiserwerth on the Lower Rhine, while the French Army looked on helpless from the left bank. Marlborough's supreme confidence in warfare always contrasted with his hesitations in politics. As soon as he took command, he assured the Dutch that he would " rid them of their troublesome neighbours " and, rapidly crossing the Meuse, he compelled the French to retreat for fear of their lines in Belgium being threatened. The manœuvre caused the two armies to converge on each other at right angles and a splendid chance of attacking the exposed flank of the French was offered. But the Dutch deputies refused to fight and risk the army that stood between their territory and the French. Four times altogether the Dutch deputies rejected opportunities of fighting in a favourable situation which Marlborough presented to them. However, the

French were outmanœuvred and were forced
impotently to watch four important fortresses on
the Meuse – Venloo, Stevenswert, Ruremonde
and Liége – fall with relatively little resistance.
The line of the Meuse as well as of the Lower
Rhine was cleared and Holland was freed from
invaders. The Dutch General Athlone was
compelled to admit that " the success of this
campaign is solely due to this incomparable
chief, since I confess that I, serving as second in
command, opposed in all circumstances his
opinions and proposals." Judged by William's
standards in the previous war, the achievement
was brilliant and Marlborough himself was alone
disappointed, for he had wanted to bring the
French to battle and not merely to take a few
fortresses.

After an adventurous journey down the Meuse,
in which he was nearly captured by a French raid-
ing party, Marlborough returned via The Hague
to England. He was enthusiastically received in
Holland, but it was nothing to his reception in
England, where his success was contrasted with the
Austrian General Eugene's failure in Italy and
the inability of Admiral Rooke to take Cadiz as
Marlborough had wished. Queen Anne raptur-
ously offered Marlborough a dukedom and £5,000
a year during her lifetime to support the dignity.
She also asked the House of Commons to grant an
income to go with the title for all time. But although the Tory majority voted with a back kick
at William III that Marlborough had " retrieved
the honour of England," they jibbed at what
they regarded as an unconstitutional request.

Marlborough, who had been urged by his wife not to accept the title unless handsome provision were made, was chagrined at the refusal, and this marked the first step in his alienation from the Tory Party.

For other reasons too he grew angry with the right-wing Tories, who were led by the Queen's uncle, Lord Rochester. He thought that Rochester was pushing too hard for purely party advantages and endangering the national effort to win the war. A wholesale attack which had been launched during the summer by the High Tories in the Cabinet on Whig J.P.s and place-holders conflicted with the " non-party " views of Marlborough and Godolphin, while the High Tory argument that the war should be waged mainly by sea and on the Spanish colonies was in contradiction to Marlborough's strategical scheme of winning the war by beating the French Army and invading France. The crying-up by this section of the Tories of Sir George Rooke's lucky feat in capturing a Spanish treasure fleet at Vigo Bay after the fiasco of Cadiz was regarded by Marlborough as a direct insult, and he was now driven to assert his influence ; when Rochester refused to go to Dublin to assume his office as Viceroy, Marlborough drove him from the Cabinet.

On top of the Tory manœuvres, the Dutch obstructions and the Whig intrigues of his wife came the most personal blow of all to Marlborough when in February, 1703, his only surviving son John, a youth of sixteen at Cambridge, died of smallpox. Marlborough returned to Holland in the early spring of 1703 with a heavy heart.

The dynast in him was sorely disappointed. Power, money and glory had been accumulated, but for what? " I've lost what is so dear to me," he murmured in one of his spells of depression. " It is fit for me to retire and not toil and labour for I know not who." But he was soon to smell the joy of battle again.

The war was now spreading to the farthest corners of Europe and over every quarter the English commander cast his perspicacious eye. In spite of Rooke's failure at Cadiz, Marlborough continued to urge the allied navies to seek a base in the Mediterranean so that France might be distracted in the south. At the same time he pressed for money and assistance to be sent to the French Protestants, who had risen against Louis XIV in the west of France. This move was a natural counter to Louis's own successful efforts at stirring up insurrection among the Magyar subjects of the Emperor, who were disturbing Vienna from the rear. Louis also now effected another diplomatic coup when with lavish promises he persuaded the Elector of Bavaria, one of the most powerful princes in Germany, to join his side. On account of the Elector's defection the French decided to make their principal effort in the 1703 campaign on the Upper Rhine, and Hector de Villars, the ablest French general, was dispatched to join forces with the Bavarians. Before the normal winter suspension of operations was ended, he began his campaign by taking the town of Kehl. Marshal Villeroi, in command in Flanders, was also inspired to retake Liége, if he could, early in the campaigning season, but otherwise to act on the defensive and hold the allied forces so as to prevent them from assisting the harassed Emperor.

Marlborough, however, was also early in the field and at first hoped that he might be allowed to draw off pressure from the Emperor by invading Belgium, even at the risk of a battle with Villeroi. But the Dutch maintained their veto on battles, and asked the Duke instead to take Bonn on the Rhine in order to clear their communications with the Empire. Under Marlborough's personal supervision that town was bombarded into surrender so quickly that Villeroi had no time to make a counter-move. Marlborough, ever fruitful in expedient, now proposed to the Dutch what he termed his " Grand Design," a remarkable strategical scheme which marks the heights of his military genius. His plan was that he himself would hold Villeroi's main army immobile whilst one Dutch general, Cohorn, attacked Ostend, another menaced Antwerp from the west and a third approached from the north-east. If the Governor of Antwerp divided his forces to save Ostend, Antwerp would fall and, if not, Ostend would. But Marlborough reckoned without his collaborators. Cohorn calmly obtained permission from the Dutch Government to alter his orders so as to turn his part into a mere plundering expedition. Opdam, one of the other Dutch generals, began his move before any diversion of forces from Antwerp had taken place and then omitted to fortify his line. Consequently his army was caught by the French in superior numbers and

Opdam ran away thinking it would be crushed. His second-in-command retrieved the error (battle of Eckeren, July 2) and Marlborough unjustly got the blame even from the Dutch. Ten days later Marlborough again created an opportunity by manœuvring Villeroi out of his lines, but the Dutch were now far too frightened to consent easily to a battle, and while they debated the chance was lost. So for the remainder of a disappointing campaign Marlborough had to be content with the capture of two petty fortresses, Huy below Liége on the Meuse (August 25) and Limburg, which was then Spanish territory (September 27). Under the terms of the Grand Alliance, both the Dutch and the Emperor's representative claimed the right to administer Limburg, and Marlborough had to arrange a clever but temporary compromise. After the fall of Limburg he sourly observed that he " was not fond of staying with an army that does nothing but eat forage," and returned to England as soon as he could.

Marlborough's claims to be a great statesman and diplomatist would stand higher if he had exerted himself as actively over far-reaching decisions of national policy as he did over matters in which the strength of the Army or the working unity of his military alliance was directly concerned. His attitude to the treaty with Portugal, which had been concluded in May, 1703, is a case in point. He had long pressed for an alliance with Portugal so as to secure Lisbon as a base for the English Navy, but seems to have been indifferent to the terms of the Treaty. Yet one of its terms

was of fundamental importance for the future of
the war. In order to obtain the assistance of the
allied forces in an attack on his country's traditional enemy, Spain, the King of Portugal had
managed to induce the English Government to
extend its war aims to include not merely com-
pensation for the Emperor, as laid down by the
Treaty of the Grand Alliance, but also an astonishing clause that " no peace shall be made till
the House of Austria be in possession of the whole
monarchy of Spain." The Dutch naturally hated
this clause being forced upon them ; it meant an
indefinite prolongation of the war, it tilted the
balance of power decisively in favour of the Habsburgs, and the Emperor, for whose presumed
benefit the clause was added, showed himself
most reluctant to send his son to Spain. Yet there
is no indication in his letters that Marlborough
protested or even inquired about a clause which
was entirely contrary to the original aims of the
Grand Alliance and was indeed to contribute in
the end to his downfall. All he objected to then
was that he had to part with some of his troops
and send them to the Peninsula.

The High Tories joined hands with the ex-
tremist Whigs in censoring Marlborough for his
ill-success in the campaign of 1703. Godolphin
grumbled that, though he was indifferent to
" the hot men of either party," the obstruc-
tionism of the Dutch " gives too just a handle
for clamour against our great expense of carrying
on this war in their country." Dutch non-co-
operation, Villars' deep penetration into Germany, which even menaced Vienna, and the

continued incompetence of the English Navy
had combined to make the war situation so
unfavourable that Godolphin expected the
Government would be torn to pieces. Further
fuel was added to the flames of Marlborough's ire
because the Dutch failed to give effect to their
promise to cease trade with France, and, while
the Whigs sniffed at his operations, his wife
continued to advocate their wider representation
in the Cabinet. In all the circumstances it was
not so surprising that he spoke of " retiring from
these uneasy and troublesome broils " as that he
was persuaded to retain his command without
any reconstruction of the Cabinet. But his
patience proved wise, for the High Tories pro-
voked Anne personally and in the course of the
following year she dismissed their representatives
in the Cabinet, although as yet no more Whigs
entered the Government.

CHAPTER IV

THE CONQUERING HERO : 1704

The march to the Danube – battle of the Schellenberg – devastation of Bavaria – relations with Eugene – battle of Blenheim – rewards and consequences – return to the Moselle.

At the end of the second campaign of the war the position of the Grand Alliance was critical. True, thanks to Marlborough, the Dutch Republic was safe, but England's third ally, the Emperor, was in desperate danger. Magyar rebels were within twenty miles of Vienna on the east, whilst, owing to the defection of the Elector of Bavaria, the French were on the line of the Danube stretching from Ulm to Linz, within a few days' march of Vienna, with an army twice the size of the Austrians. Thus at the very moment when the English Government was promising to put the Archduke Charles on the throne of Madrid, his father, the Emperor Leopold, was tottering on his throne at Vienna. In the centre of the vast war front the French had also advanced and, by the capture of Landau and other fortresses, held a strong position on the Upper Rhine. Here their troops were faced by Imperialists under the Margrave Louis of Baden, whose methods of warfare were slow and antiquated and who was thought in Vienna to be capable of following the Elector of Bavaria into the French camp. In Italy, though, owing to the success of the Sea Powers, a new ally had been gained in the Duke of Savoy-Piedmont, the Imperialists were in no way able to resist the French. The immense French front therefore stretched (outside Italy) in the form of a ladder inclined to the left of the European map, with its top resting near Antwerp and its foot on the Danube.

Marlborough was filled with gloom at this outlook. In the course of the winter he reached the conclusion that the only way in which the Alliance could be saved was for him to make a personal effort to rescue the Emperor. Direct appeals had reached him from Vienna, and they well accorded with his mood of resentment against the Dutch. In January he told the Imperial Ambassador Extraordinary, Wratislaw, that he intended to induce the Dutch to agree to a move on the Upper Rhine or the Moselle whereby he might assist the overthrow of the Elector of Bavaria ; but he added that he could not hope to employ more troops than the number which were actually English or in English pay. His daring decision to separate the Dutch and English Armies and to carry the latter away from the northern theatre of war was the first stage in the courageous scheme which he finally evolved for a march as far as the Danube. As spring approached, it gradually became plain to him that a threat to invade France by way of Lorraine from the Moselle might not save Vienna, and that more far-reaching remedies were needed. In April he obtained authorization in general terms from the Queen to separate the two armies and to use the English troops to aid the Empire.

DM

He asked that Prince Eugene, the best Imperialist general, should be sent to the Upper Rhine, and he sowed in Dutch minds the idea of a campaign on the Moselle so as to induce them to lend him at least a portion of their troops to act away from their frontiers. But although all the necessary preparations were made for a march south, it was not until the spring was well advanced that he finally decided on the bold hazard of a six-hundred-mile flank march down to the Danube to knock out the Elector of Bavaria and save Vienna.

At the beginning of May he disclosed his intentions to Godolphin. He told Wratislaw that " the issue in this matter is victory or death," but he also said in more cheerful mood " the more I think of the expedition the better I am pleased with it." On May 19, after he had reviewed what he called his " little army " of some 50,000 men (of whom 16,000 were English), the extraordinary enterprise began. For its success he had to create a fog of war to deceive the French, lest they barred his path or cut his supplies. He managed to persuade them first that he intended to invade Lorraine and then, as he moved farther up the Rhine, that he was going to attack Alsace. Not until he left the line of the Rhine for a sharp turn east below the Neckar valley by way of Heidelberg was his real intention revealed to the enemy, and not till then were the Dutch authorities and German princes officially informed of his destination. He deceived not only the French but many of his own allies, and yet he did this without in any

way hustling or weakening his troops on the
march. They plodded methodically on. Marlborough and the cavalry went ahead, his brother,
General Charles Churchill, with the infantry
behind. They went forward at a steady rate of
ten miles a day, setting out at sunrise and encamp-
ing about midday. " Surely," wrote an English
captain, "never was such a march carried on
with more order and regularity and with less
fatigue both to man and horse." The soldiers
enjoyed the expedition. The interfering Dutch
field deputies were left behind and, although
the States General at first appealed to the
Duke in terror to return, they soon realized that
he was carrying the war with him, for Villeroi,
the French general in Holland, was compelled
to follow him, and the Dutch then of their own
accord sent reinforcements after him. At length,
on June 10 at Gross-Heppach on the road to the
Danube, the Duke, Prince Eugene and the
Margrave of Baden foregathered to concert
operations. After a magnificent banquet, it was
arranged that Eugene with 30,000 men should
station himself on the Rhine to watch the French
generals Villeroi and Tallard, who commanded
the army there, while Marlborough and the
Margrave should move together into Bavaria.
On June 22 Marlborough and the Margrave
joined forces on the edge of the Swabian Jura
Mountains north-west of Ulm. The command
over this joint force of 80,000 had been delicately
settled beforehand. Baden as a prince was of
higher rank than Marlborough, but the Emperor
promised that Marlborough's views on strategy

should be decisive although the two generals
were to enjoy the honour of giving the actual
orders and issuing the password on alternate
days. It would indeed have been ludicrous for
Marlborough to have come all this tedious way
unless he had first obtained a guarantee that his
wishes would be respected. Moreover, he had
the address to work smoothly with the touchy
Margrave. On July 1, as they approached the
Danube, he proposed to him that they should
storm the fortress of the Schellenberg which lay
beside the town of Donauwörth in order that
they might cross the Danube into the heart of
Bavaria and threaten its capital, Munich ; the
Margrave agreed. This plan meant that the
attack could not be launched until late on the
morrow, after the troops had marched fifteen
miles, and also that a frontal onslaught would
have to be made on a well-fortified position
guarded by veteran Bavarian troops. But there
were three advantages in the hurried move.
First, that of a surprise, since the Bavarian commander, Count D'Arco, would not expect an
attack so soon ; secondly, the fortifications to
the west were incomplete and could not be completed by that time ; thirdly, if there were delay,
Marsin, the French general on the Danube, and
the Elector of Bavaria, whose army was only
some twenty miles away, would be able to send
reinforcements. Marlborough asked his troops
for this tremendously unorthodox exertion since
delay would mean, he asserted, " either the
enemy will escape or will have time to finish
their works." It was these factors and not the

half-legendary story of the alternation of the command which caused the battle of the Schellenberg to be fought on July 2, 1704.

As the fortress was situated between the Danube and an impenetrable wood, only two main lines of attack were open, from the north-west and the west. Although, or because, the fortifications to the west were the weakest, Marlborough took command of the English troops who were to deliver a storm on the " death angle " near the wood from the north-west. After a forced march along bad roads, picked battalions began the attack at six in the evening. At first the Bavarians threw them back with ease and inflicted heavy losses ; General Goor, the Dutchman on whom Marlborough greatly depended, was shot dead in the first charge. But the fierce pummelling which his forces received at this point obliged D'Arco to divert men from the west, while the commander at Donauwörth disgracefully neglected to man his palisades. In consequence, the Margrave of Baden, although met by an enfilading fire, found less difficulty. While Marlborough was hammering at the north-west, he " walked into " the fortress on the west ; it was an obvious case of cause and effect, although Marlborough's detractors did not fail to allege that the " experienced " Margrave had shown himself more astute than his colleague.

The capture of the Schellenberg was an expensive victory for those days. The Allies had 1,500 men killed and 4,500 wounded, and over a quarter of the English engaged were casualties. The

Bavarians probably had about the same number of casualties, but barely 5,000 of D'Arco's troops escaped to join the Elector. An English officer who took part described it as "a considerable advantage purchased at a dear rate rather than a victory." Marlborough himself confessed that the action was "a little expensive." Was the conquest worth the price ? The lie of the country suggests that the Schellenberg could not have been masked and that swift progress into Bavaria was barred unless it were taken. The question is whether Marlborough was wise to hurry. Alone among Marlborough's biographers, his latest is a little hesitant in allotting praise. "It is arguable," writes Mr. Winston Churchill,

> though by no means provable, that if he had waited till the 3rd and brought the whole army into play on both sides of the wood, the enemy even though reinforced could not have held so extended a line and possibly life might have been spared. But the fear of reinforcements was decisive upon him.

The days which followed the victory of the Schellenberg were in the nature of an anti-climax for Marlborough, as he was neither able to besiege Munich nor to bring the Franco-Bavarian army to battle. The Emperor, although lavish in his congratulations, had been parsimonious in providing siege guns, while Marsin and the Elector took up an impregnable position at Augsburg. Marlborough crossed the Danube, after occupying two small fortresses the better to clear his communications across the river, and encamped for ten days at Friedburg, where he faced his enemy. At this period there was a hope that the

Elector of Bavaria might be induced to abandon the French alliance. By way of warning him of the consequences of refusal and in spite of the protests of his colleague, the Margrave of Baden, Marlborough ordered that Bavaria should be be laid waste save so far as this affected the supplies of his own army. Hundreds of villages were set on fire, barns destroyed, stocks seized and a plentiful harvest was prevented from being reaped. Various reasons were assigned by Marlborough for this terrible devastation. In a letter of July 16, he wrote that it was " in order to get the Elector to hearken to terms," but on July 29 he said " it was to deprive the enemy as well of his present subsistence as future support on this side." Between the two dates, however, it had become obvious that the Elector had made up his mind to stick to the French and probably the devastation begun for one reason was continued for another. Marlborough wrote twice to his wife deploring the burnings as " contrary to my nature," but, nevertheless, he ordered them to be continued and indeed extended.

One reason why the Elector of Bavaria had refused to negotiate with the Allies was the news that Marshal Tallard had left the Rhine and was coming to his help. Prince Eugene, who had remained on the Rhine to keep watch against both Tallard and Villeroi, was unable to prevent Tallard's departure but, leaving two-thirds of his own army behind to watch Villeroi, followed him to the Danube. Much has been written about the close and spontaneous friendship between the fiery, French-hating Eugene and

Marlborough when they met for the first time at
Gross-Heppach and became "two bodies with
one soul." In the long run, no doubt, a real
friendship was attained through their comrade-
ship in arms. But it would be a mistake to
imagine that this first month of contact was a
perfect honeymoon. Eugene was very critical
of Marlborough's strategy after the fall of the
Schellenberg. The credit for taking the fortress
he believed was due to the Dutch General Goor
and Marlborough's failure to achieve anything
substantial in these July days Eugene attributed
to Goor's death on the battlefield. He argued
that Marlborough should have forced the Elector
to battle at Augsburg by cutting his communications and that he ought at least to have prevented
the junction with Tallard. Marlborough, for
his part, at the same time thought that it was
Eugene's business to prevent this junction. "I
depend very much on the vigilance of Prince
Eugene," he told Godolphin, "for should Tallard
join the Elector it would draw the business to a
greater length than is for the good of the country."
However, Tallard did join the Elector south of
the Danube on August 7, and on August 11
Eugene joined Marlborough some miles farther
down the river. Before this and in spite of their
desire to fight a battle, Marlborough and Eugene
allowed the Margrave of Baden to take off
15,000 men to lay siege to Ingoldstadt. They
preferred to dispense with an embarrassing
colleague even at the cost of weakening their
forces.

The united French forces, which numbered

about 4,000 men more than the Allies without the Margrave (56,000 against 52,000) and were superior in artillery, did not expect to be attacked. On the night of August 12 they were entrenched in a strong position which stretched four miles from the Danube to the woods farther north. On the right of their line was the tiny village of Blenheim, in which Tallard posted nine battalions with eighteen battalions in support. The centre of the French line was protected by the deepish and muddy Nebel stream and was less strongly held. Tallard, in fact, believed that the stream constituted so dangerous an obstacle to his enemy that the Allied troops could be freely permitted to cross it and could then be driven back into it. On the left of the French line was concentrated the original army of Marsin and the Elector, with the village of Ober Glauheim on their right. Such were the French dispositions which Marlborough and Eugene determined to assault on the morning of August 13, 1704. They achieved an important moral surprise by attacking at all, but the delay involved in the elaborate deployment of their army (about four and a half hours) gave the French ample time for their preparations. It was arranged that Eugene should command on the Allied right facing Marsin and the Elector, while Marlborough should take charge on the centre and left. On his left the Duke put Lord Cutts with sixteen battalions to deal with the twenty-seven French battalions in or around Blenheim. Eugene was likewise markedly inferior in numbers to his opponents on the French left. Thus Marlborough was left with a preponderance of force, which he could and did in fact use in the centre.

The battle opened with a fierce but unavailing onslaught on Blenheim by the English troops, similar to their assault on the " death angle " at the Schellenberg. But after two hours Marlborough ordered Cutts to desist and be content with " containing " (holding) the enemy. At the same time Eugene had been repulsed at the other end of the line, while Marsin, an able general, who evidently either did not know or care about Tallard's preconceived ideas, ordered a flank attack from Ober Glauheim on Marlborough's centre as it began to struggle across the the Nebel stream. Eleven battalions, including the Irish in French service, executed a brilliant charge which, had it been followed up sufficiently quickly, might have reversed the result of the battle. Marlborough galloped to the threatened spot, threw in his reserves and appealed to Eugene for cavalry. This was the crisis. Eugene, though hard pressed, responded promptly, a dangerous counter-move was repulsed and by 4.30 in the afternoon Marlborough's forces were all safely across the Nebel. As the result of the sustained efforts of Eugene and Cutts on the right and left, the French were incapacitated from concentrating any flanking movement such as Tallard had planned against the Allied centre. At the crucial point, Marlborough had eighty squadrons and twenty-three battalions against fifty squadrons and nine battalions in the French centre. Thus after seven hours' fighting Marlborough saw that he had won. The nine French battalions, consisting mainly of young soldiers, made one heroic counter-charge, but numbers told and at about 5.30 in the evening a final Allied charge decided the battle. Tallard himself was captured trying to fetch assistance from Blenheim.

Marlborough hastened to scribble a note on the back of a tavern bill to carry the news of the " glorious victory " to his wife. Marsin and the Elector, on hearing that the centre was broken, withdrew their troops in fairly good order and even counter-charged as they withdrew, but on the right twenty-seven battalions, who through the stupidity of their commander had all been drawn into and cramped helplessly in Blenheim village, were bluffed into surrender. Thus the Allies captured some 15,000 prisoners besides inflicting about 23,000 casualties. The Allied losses were over 12,000 and they were too exhausted to pursue the French left.

The battle of Blenheim was one of the most immediately decisive battles in European history. It was the first time that the French had suffered defeat for over two generations. It saved Vienna and conquered Bavaria. It assured the ultimate aggrandizement of the House of Austria and was a final check to the territorial ambitions of Louis XIV beyond the Rhine. It was also a blow to the House of Stuart and enabled Marlborough and Godolphin's Coalition Ministry to stay in office for another four years.

Marlborough had his material rewards. Queen Anne allotted to him the royal manor of Woodstock, on the site of which Sir John

Vanbrugh was to build Blenheim Palace at the
nation's expense. He was also made a Prince
of the Holy Roman Empire, although the
economical Emperor was careful to give him
only fifteen square miles of territory at Mindelheim to support the honour, and this territory,
being filched from the conquered Elector of
Bavaria, was certain to become the matter of dispute when peace negotiations were opened. It
was typical of Marlborough that, just as he
refused to accept his dukedom until he was
given an income to support it, he would not take
his title of prince until he was given a principality.

After the battle of Blenheim the Danubian city
of Ulm was recaptured and the Margrave of
Baden, a little disconsolate at being left out at
Blenheim, returned to the Rhine to besiege and
take Landau for the second time, a feat which he
achieved with the maximum of incompetence.
Marlborough grew weary of covering this drawn-
out siege and carried his own forces back to the
Moselle, where he surprised Trèves and arranged
for the capture of Trarbach with a view to an
invasion of France along this valley in the next
campaigning season. But his own toils even then
were not at an end. He reluctantly agreed to an
800-mile journey to Berlin and back in order to persuade the King of Prussia not to divert his troops
from the Central European war to a war which
was in progress in the north. Thus it was not
until the middle of December that the fifty-four-
year-old conquering hero, unutterably weary,
could reach London to savour the gratitude of his
Queen and country.

CHAPTER V

MILITARY GENIUS

Marlborough as tactician and strategist – views on naval power –
the blind spot of Spain.

MARLBOROUGH's first three campaigns as Commander-in-Chief of the English Army had shown
him to possess ideas about the tactical and
strategical problems of warfare very different
from those of his predecessors. In the first place,
it was his consistent view, as he wrote to Godolphin
in 1703, that " if we cannot bring the French to
a battle, we shall not do anything worth being
commended." This emphasis on the importance
of seeking battle was something comparatively
new in the military conceptions of his generation. From the closing years of the Thirty
Years' War a preference for defensive warfare
and big sieges rather than a showdown between
two armies had prevailed in Europe. The
French general, Turenne, was a rare exception to
a run of Continental commanders (including
William III and Louis XIV) who liked to avoid
pitched battles. It is to be remarked that Marlborough served as a young man under Turenne
and was commended by him for his exceptional
qualities. That Marlborough learned something
from Turenne can hardly be questioned.

But to seek battle was one thing ; to attain it
quite another. In those days not only did it
take two to make a fight, but the evasion of

battle did not necessarily mean headlong retreat.
The French were invariably able to retire, if
they preferred to do so, to a strong prepared
position where they could not be assailed, while
the mobility of Marlborough's armies was not
such as to make simple the task of catching the
French in an unfavourable position, and the
lengthy and tedious business of deploying in
battle formation afforded frequent opportunities
for escape. Marlborough therefore had to resort
to methods of surprise to force the French to
fight as an alternative to a humiliating retreat,
and it was his employment of surprise rather
than his consistent habit of seeking battle that
is the supreme proof of his genius.

To the actual tactical dispositions for battle
Marlborough made several novel contributions.
He revived Cromwell's and Rupert's use of the
cavalry as a shock instead of a missile weapon.
The early seventeenth-century custom had been
to allow the cavalry after going into the fray to
halt and deliver musket fire, thereby throwing
away the advantage of their superior speed.
Marlborough had his cavalry move at a brisk
trot, fight in a line three deep as under Cromwell
and Rupert, and use the sword as their exclusive
weapon. According to Colonel Kane, who
fought in his army, the Duke " would allow
the horse [cavalrymen] but three charges of
powder and ball to each man for a campaign,
and that only for guarding their horses when at
grass and not to be made use of in action."
With his infantry, on the contrary, he laid primary
stress on the correct employment of firearms.

The invention of the ring bayonet, which was fully introduced into the English Army in 1703, got rid of the distinction which existed in Cromwell's army between musketeers and pikemen, for the two were henceforward combined. Moreover, the supersession of clumsier methods of loading by the general use of the flintlock enabled Marlborough to attain from musketry a concentration of fire power never before known. He insisted upon the importance of fire discipline in the infantry and established firing by platoons instead of by ranks so as to enable the platoon commander to direct the volleys and to maintain a more regular fire than the French. Likewise, Marlborough recognized the value of artillery, although cannon were still in a comparatively primitive state. He selected able artillery commanders, but always retained for himself the personal direction of the artillery in battle. He sent his orders to his brigadiers without any intermediary ; at Blenheim he took personal charge of placing his cannon and at Ramillies he was to give it an unusually urgent rôle on the left wing. Shock tactics with the cavalry, disciplined fire in the infantry, personal care of the artillery—these were the three main factors in Marlborough's tactical success.

In battle tactics Marlborough demonstrated his brilliant unorthodoxy at Blenheim (and later at Oudenarde). Here was none of the traditional elaborate manœuvring in the face of the enemy, but a deliberately worked-out original plan. His move against the centre at Blenheim was one not recognized in any contemporary

text-book of war. For it was generally
assumed in seventeenth-century military circles
that such an attack would be overwhelmed by
the enemy's wings. Marlborough, however, first
made certain that the French wings were well
held and then gave his decisive order to break
through the centre. There was nothing rash in
this, no uncalculated risks, no brutal trifling with
his soldiers' lives here or ever. And so when he
asked his men for a special effort they gave it
willingly.

Marlborough had a marked perception of the
value of sea power. Having served on board the
Fleet as a subaltern and held a commission in the
Marines, he knew the difficulties and limitations
of naval warfare. His only notable mistake in
regard to sea power was that he expected too
much of a projected naval raid on the western
coast of France in 1708, while neglecting to give
the naval commanders adequate information
about the situation of the French forces in the
neighbourhood. On the other hand, he was constantly and rightly urging upon the admirals the
need of obtaining a base where the Fleet could
winter in the Mediterranean. " I conjure you if
possible to take Port Mahon [Minorca]," he
wrote to General Stanhope in 1708, and it was
not his fault that this valuable base was not
conquered before that year.

Although nearly all Marlborough's fighting
was done in Flanders, nothing is more striking
than his power of seeing the vast coalition as a
whole. In his dispatches, we see him following
distant events and relating them to each other

with a consummate grasp of synthesis. His march to the Danube in 1704 and his proposed march to Italy in 1705 were in their daring simplicity strokes of true strategic genius. Never in military matters did he allow his direct concern in the war close at hand to dominate his mind. " I am sensible," he told Godolphin in 1704, " that if I did not consider the good of the whole before my private concern, I ought not to be here." In constantly relating one campaign to another, he perceived the virtue of an economy of forces ; how a defensive in the Netherlands meant an offensive elsewhere ; alternatively, how if the enemy could be held with small numbers in Germany, he could do what he liked in the Netherlands. In a debate in which he took part in 1707, he defended his concentration of forces in Flanders on the ground that, if the pressure were relaxed there, large numbers of French troops would be released from garrison duty to fight in campaigns elsewhere, whereas since in Spain the French were able to garrison their strong places with only one battalion, to shift the main Allied military effort to Spain would be to violate grossly the principle of economizing their own forces.

But strategically Marlborough did have one real weakness and that was in regard to the war in Spain, although for opposite reasons from those urged against him by his political enemies. He had advocated and supported the extension of the Allied war aims to the conquest of Spain for the benefit of the Habsburgs, and never seems to have understood the tremendous prolongation of

E M

the war which was involved in this expensive and difficult project. He once confessed that he did not have time to read all the letters and dispatches from Spain and Portugal. Perhaps in consequence he never appreciated the stubborn guerilla qualities and ineradicable partisanship of the Spanish people or the vast geographical obstacles to military progress on the Peninsula. He always insisted that he himself must remain near Holland, partly because, if he left, the Dutch might be induced to conclude a separate peace. But while he refused to go to Spain himself, to meet the wishes of the Whig Party, who largely for economic reasons were rabid for the French overthrow in Spain, he allowed his forces to be divided, thereby weakening his chances of invading France from the north-east and at the same time allowing inferior troops in the charge of quarrelsome generals to be constantly defeated in Spain. Moreover he did not realize that the Spanish people had made their choice and that he was required to subdue a people as well as an army. On the issue of Spain, he allowed political considerations to cloud his clear military judgment ; and it is possible that it was of Spain that he was thinking in the last days of life when aged, paralysed and in virtual retirement as Commander-in-Chief, he was asked for his advice and could be induced to utter only four words : " Don't divide the army."

CHAPTER VI

GLOOM AND CHEER : 1705–1706

Cabinet reconstruction and general election – the " Triumvirate " – disappointing campaign of 1705 – battle of Ramillies – conquest of Belgium – Allied differences – offer of Governor-Generalship.

THE victories on the Danube excited the patriotic enthusiasm of the English people, but the High Tories, now that their leaders had left the Cabinet, were distinctly dissatisfied. Rochester said that the losses of the French armies at Blenheim were no more than a bucketful of water to the French King, and the Tory majority in the Commons insisted on coupling the name of Sir George Rooke with that of Marlborough in the congratulatory address, because Rooke, more by luck than judgment, had that August conquered the Rock of Gibraltar and fought a drawn battle with the French off Malaga. When Marlborough offered Rooke a free ticket for a dinner given to him by the City of London, Rooke pointedly refused and became so antagonistic to the Ministry that the Queen was compelled to dismiss him. In the domestic field the extreme Tories again tried to force through an Occasional Conformity Bill, aimed at excluding the Nonconformists from political life, which had twice been defeated in earlier sessions. But they were defeated by their own moderates in the Commons, while the Bill was again rejected by the Lords, and Marlborough, who had previously voted for it, now voted against it. With these straws to show how the political winds blew, Marlborough now decided that the effective continuation of the war, his one concern, required a reconstructed administration based solely on moderate Whigs and moderate Tories. He personally demanded the Privy Seal of another High Tory, the Duke of Buckinghamshire, and handed it to an influential and wealthy Whig, the Duke of Newcastle (April, 1705).

At the General Election which followed, the Queen was induced to use her influence against the extreme Tories and the result was to increase the number of Whigs and " Queen's Servants," or non-party men, in the House of Commons at the expense of the Tories. Sarah had pressed on her husband the advisability of capitulating entirely to the Whigs in their hungry search of office, but he told her frankly that he believed it to be best for " the Queen's service," i.e. for the war, that " neither party should have a great majority, so that both might be influenced for her interest."

The reconstructed Government was based firmly on what was called the " Triumvirate " of Marlborough, Godolphin and Robert Harley, the moderate Tory leader who had become principal Secretary of State in 1704. But after the election the " Triumvirate " in fact became dependent on the support of the well-organized Whig party, and before the year was out they were forced to throw a sop to that party by appointing one of its five leaders, Lord Sunderland, who also happened to be Marlborough's son-in-law, Ambassador Extraordinary in Vienna. While the election was in progress, Marlborough had sailed for the front in a cheerful mood. In the course of the election he was attacked for betraying the Church of England, but he knew that his victories counted more with the electorate than his views on occasional conformity.

The disaster on the Danube compelled Louis XIV to act on the defensive in 1705. By tremendous exertions he assembled three large armies to stand guard against the expected invasion of French or Spanish territory from the east ; one army was under Villeroi in Flanders, a second under Villars on the Moselle and a third under Marsin in Alsace. Marlborough had made up his mind to try to invade Lorraine by way of the Moselle, as he regarded this as the " real road " into France. His plan was to begin the advance with two armies, one of 60,000 men under his own command from Trèves which he had taken at the end of the previous campaign, the other of 30,000 Germans under the Margrave of Baden operating from Landau on the Upper Rhine. But a fatal combination of Dutch fears, Austrian shortcomings, Prussian dilatoriness and the Margrave's jealousy prevented the realization of what seems in any case to have been an over-ambitious project. Nevertheless, Marlborough refused wholly to abandon it. Ultimately he decided to confront Villars, who had taken up an impregnable position, with an inferior army in the hope of tempting him to give battle. But Villars was too clever to take an unnecessary risk. For fifteen days Marlborough encamped opposite him in a neighbourhood where the Allies had no adequate source of supplies. Every night there were hard frosts, men deserted and there was no proper commissariat. The Duke was sick with disappointment and confessed that "nothing would do good except a battle" and that he could not have. The would-be invaders of France were compelled to retreat of their own accord. So disgusted was Marlborough that he took the unusual step of sending a message to Marshal Villars, apologizing for giving him "poor sport" and putting the blame on the Margrave's refusal to co-operate.

Villeroi, in the absence of Marlborough from Flanders, retook the fortress of Huy and attacked Liége. This gave Marlborough an admirable excuse for disentangling himself from a humiliating situation. But the Dutch were too delighted with his return to complain ; he at once recaptured Huy, although he told his wife despondently that "the Lord knows what we shall do next." Meanwhile the German commander at Trèves had pusillanimously abandoned the town and Villars had advanced and driven the Imperialists from their lines. No wonder that Marlborough wrote "I am weary of life" and announced once again his intention of retiring at the close of the campaign.

To those who are accustomed to regard Marlborough as a serene Olympian figure his conduct during this disappointing campaign of 1705 should be especially revealing. For the plain truth is that he was no more philosophical than any other man and equally prone to fits of depression when defeated or thwarted. In 1704 he had set out in a state of complete depression because of what had happened in the previous year, and in 1705 he had been optimistic for the same reason. When his allies disappointed him, he threatened to resign, and he used strong language and stronger action against the men who obstructed his military schemes. He was as sensitive to criticism as any other public man, but he chose to redeem his character with his sword.

In midsummer, 1705, he decided that if he could not count on the assistance of his allies to carry through his plans of campaign he must repeat the tactics adopted in the march to the Danube and bluff the Dutch into victory. His feat in breaking through the carefully prepared lines erected in Brabant by Villeroi was the march to the Danube in miniature. He persuaded the Dutch generals and field deputies who now rejoined him that he had only reconnaissance objects in view. But by swift night marches, carried out solely by the troops in English pay, he so feinted at the French lines and so befogged the French general that he broke through at the weak point of Tirlemont with the loss of only 200 men (July 29). He led the crucial charge himself and was nearly killed when a French cavalry officer tried to sabre him but fell off his horse. Marlborough reported to Godolphin, with a slight touch of malice, that the Dutch did not reach the lines until the action was all over and that he had been forced to " cheat " them into following him at all.

But afterwards caution overcame him. He

refused to pursue the advantage for fear that the
whole French army were coming up to repair the
breach in their lines. Had he done so he would
almost certainly have inflicted a severe defeat on
a section of the French infantry and taken the
vital town of Louvain. But he, who earlier in the
campaign had been ready to fight Villars with
inferior numbers far from his base, now held his
hand. Such was the effect of the depressed mood
induced by his failure on the Moselle. And yet
here is the astonishing thing – with this small, if
striking, success behind him the mood of caution
was quickly overcome. A few days later he
manœuvred Villeroi into such a position that he
was compelled to surrender Louvain if he were
to save Brussels, but, instead of racing for Brussels,
Marlborough tried to persuade the Dutch deputies
to agree to a battle roughly on the site of the later
battlefield of Waterloo. A majority of the Dutch
generals, led by the choleric Slangenberg, refused
assent, just as they had refused to fight on an
earlier and less favourable occasion twelve days
after the passage of the lines. Marlborough was
bitterly disappointed. For his forces at Waterloo
were greater by one-third than those of his enemy,
and he assured Godolphin that he would have had
a bigger victory than Blenheim if he had possessed
supreme powers.

Once again the Duke yielded momentarily to
anger and disappointment. When the English
Government, for obvious political reasons, sup-
pressed a passage in the *Official Gazette* which
would have disclosed to the world how the Dutch
had obstructed a victory, he exclaimed : " I am

very sure I must be madder than anybody in
Bedlam if I should be desirous of serving when I
am sure that my enemies seek my destruction and
my friends sacrifice my honour to their wisdom."
He protested violently to the Dutch at the behaviour of their generals and obtained the dismissal of Slangenberg. But he allowed himself
as usual to be persuaded to continue in office,
gratified by the assurances of Queen Anne and
the new Emperor Joseph (elder brother of the
Archduke Charles) and by the spontaneous burst
of enthusiasm in Holland itself. He exerted
himself to prevent the Dutch discussing with the
French peace terms which might involve their
recognizing Louis XIV's grandson as King of
Spain, and he started for Vienna to clear up a
quarrel with Berlin " by a great many good
words " and to concert with the new Emperor
plans for the next campaign.

Marlborough passed the winter of 1705-6 in
comparative peace. The Whigs, who saw their
chance had come, were content to bide their time
and demonstrate their indispensability to the
Government. In January Lord Halifax, one of
the Whig chiefs, invited Marlborough, Godolphin,
Sunderland and eight leading City merchants to
dinner and thereby successfully opened the campaign to raise £250,000 as a loan to assist the
Austrian invasion of Italy. Here, in contrast to
Spain and Belgium, the Allies' position was desperate and Marlborough not merely subscribed,
but contemplated marching in person to the help
of Prince Eugene and repeating the triumphs of his

Danube campaign on the banks of the Po. He
had the Queen's consent and sent his Quarter-
master, Cadogan, to obtain permission to lead the
German and Scandinavian troops into Italy.
This plan was finally thwarted early in May, 1706,
by a successful French offensive in Germany,
which forced Louis of Baden to retreat from his
lines and frightened the Dutch. Marlborough
therefore had to content himself with sending
Eugene a reinforcement of 10,000 men and planning an English naval diversion on the coast of
France which might draw off troops from the
Italian and German fronts. For he was confident
that the main war effort of the French would be
in Germany and Italy and that they would stand
stiffly on the defensive in Flanders. He foresaw
no glory for himself if he remained there, as he
must. Hence he returned from London to the
front once more in the grip of melancholy. But
he was mistaken. Villeroi, the French commander in Flanders, was surprisingly given
definite orders to fight.

Thus it came about that in May, 1706, Flanders
saw the unusual spectacle of two armies advancing
with intent to fight. Cadogan, sent with an
advance guard to mark out a camp, was astonished
to find the French army occupying the very position for which he himself was headed. It was a
plateau in an area covered by three streams, and
the left of the French was covered by bogs and
in particular by one of the streams, known as the
Little Geete. As at Blenheim, the French position was based on a number of hamlets, on the
left Autréglise and Offus, in the centre Ramillies

and on the right Franquenée and Taviers. The
French line spread for four miles in concave
fashion, so that the Allied line opposite formed
the arc of a chord. Marlborough, although he
believed that his forces were inferior to those of
the French (actually he was slightly superior,
especially in artillery), determined to assault the
magnificent French array. The lie of the land
gave him one considerable advantage. The fold
of a hill enabled him quickly to transfer troops
from his right to his centre or left without the
French being able to perceive the manœuvre.
On this fact he based his plan of battle.

The battle (May 23, 1706) opened on the
wings. Lord Orkney, with the English troops on
the right, managed to get across the Little Geete
and attacked the French between Autréglise and
Offus, where their finest troops were concentrated,
while the Dutch, powerfully assisted by carefully
placed cannon, at once took Fraquenée and
Taviers at the other end of the line on the left
and Ramillies was stormed by Allied infantry.
Marlborough's object was to hold the French left
with inferior numbers and to force them back
from the villages at the centre and right. By the
afternoon he was ready to begin his attack, but
the French first counter-attacked between Ramillies and their right and drove back part of the
Dutch. This was the crisis of the battle. Marlborough was prepared. He had ordered Orkney
on the right wing, much to his disgust, to draw
back from his attack and had taken from him
eighteen cavalry squadrons. While the French at
Ramillies and on the extreme right were held in

and prevented from delivering an enfilading fire, Marlborough had obtained a cavalry superiority of eighty-one squadrons against sixty-seven of the enemy at the vital point on his left centre. He now ordered up a further reserve of twenty-one squadrons, brought over from his right (all these movements of troops being concealed by the hill from the enemy). This gave him a decisive advantage of five to three. In the mêlée into which Marlborough flung himself he was nearly killed. He fell from his horse, and an aide-de-camp who held the stirrup of a fresh charger had his head blown off. Now the French cavalry broke. Villeroi vainly tried to form a fresh line on his left, but after a short breathing space Marlborough gathered his infantry, victorious at Ramillies village, linked them with the English battalions under Orkney and wheeled his whole line to the right. The French crumpled and fled, pursued remorselessly by the Allied cavalry. In the battle and pursuit the French lost 5,000 men and dared not stop until they had put the River Scheldt between themselves and their implacable enemy.

The consequences of Ramillies were more striking than those of any of Marlborough's other victories. One by one the chief Belgian towns fell, almost without resistance. Brussels, Louvain, Malines, Antwerp, Bruges and Oudenarde surrendered. Marlborough proudly reminded his wife that King William III had unsuccessfully besieged Oudenarde with 60,000 men. In vain Louis XIV stripped his other fronts in an attempt to stem the tide. In July Ostend was taken.

By August Marlborough had reached the French
frontier and laid siege to Menin in France, which
surrendered on August 22. Later, the captures of
Dendermonde and Ath put the whole of Belgium
into the hands of the Allies.

Victory presents problems almost as complex,
if not quite as severe, as those of defeat. Louis
XIV's problem was at least straightforward – to
repair as best he could the damage done and to
defend his frontiers. But with the conquest of the
Spanish Netherlands, full of valuable booty, the
Allies at once fell out among themselves. Godolphin, aware of the feeling at home, began to press
on Marlborough the need of doing something for
English interests, such as taking Dunkirk, which
was the port whence French privateers were
effectively menacing English commerce. Marlborough felt that he must not only refuse to carry
out this project immediately, but must insist that
in order to hold the alliance together England
should declare that she had no territorial ambitions in this area. The Dutch were less restrained.
They saw before their eyes the objects for which
they had mainly entered the war fully attained.
In a flash of Marlborough's sword the towns
which they coveted to form their barrier against
French aggression had become available. But
the Austrians, for their part, claimed the right to
rule Belgium as part of the Spanish Empire of
which their Archduke Charles had been acknow-
ledged by the Allies as sole heir. Marlborough
cared little for the final settlement of the rival
claims. His one aim was now to hold the alliance

together so as to be able to invade France and inflict a final crushing defeat on her. He manœuvred to this end. In June he went to The Hague and was able to arrange a compromise whereby there was to be temporarily a joint Anglo-Dutch rule over the conquered provinces but the Habsburg claims were fully guaranteed for the future. The Austrians remained uneasy and attempted to bribe the English general by offering him the Governor-Generalship of the Spanish Netherlands, in the name of the Archduke Charles, with a salary of £60,000. There is some evidence that Marlborough himself had prompted this offer as a proper payment for his work, and at first he did not expect that the Dutch would take it amiss. But a storm arose in Holland and Marlborough was compelled to refuse the tempting o.fer. He did this with some reluctance and never entirely abandoned the hope that it might be repeated at least when the war was over. The Austrians, however, were not grateful ; merely selfish. The rewards held out to him were but empty honours designed to enlist a powerful advocate. The affair was to create a permanent cleavage between Marlborough and the Dutch Government, just as the refusal of the £5,000 a year in perpetuity had split him from the English Tories.

The offer of the Governor-Generalship was not the only awkward consequence for Marlborough of the victory of Ramillies. The Dutch reasonably and naturally began to talk of peace. To him this seemed neither natural nor reasonable. This was *his* war in which he had made a big name in

Europe. Why should he abandon it before he had marched on Paris? " I am afraid," he wrote gloomily to Godolphin, " our best allies are very fond of a peace," and he instructed the Dutch generals emphatically that France was not yet reduced to her " just bounds," although what the just bounds were he omitted to tell them.

To add to his perplexities, Marlborough learned in the autumn of 1706 of political upheavals in England. Secure in their majority, the Whigs were demanding a more powerful representation in the Cabinet. They sought as the first and easiest step to make Marlborough's Whig son-in-law, Sunderland, Secretary of State. Harley, the Tory Secretary, was reluctant and Godolphin talked of resigning. Marlborough was fearful not only of losing his friend, the Treasurer, but that such dissensions in London would encourage the Dutch to seek a separate peace with France. He pleaded with Godolphin for one more year in which to " win the war." Although at first he had assured his wife (who was, of course, rabid for Sunderland) that " a villainous race of vipers was planning to make the Queen uneasy at home " and that Sunderland was unsuited to a Secretary-ship of State, by the autumn he had changed his tune. He begged Godolphin to stay in office and to convert Harley to accepting the Whig terms. In October he pleaded with the stubborn Queen to be governed " by the only party which will rally in support of her measures" – a very different tone from his non-party professions of 1702 and later. Eventually the Queen unwillingly gave way. In December Sunderland became

Secretary and the Queen attended the baptism of his second son, of whom Marlborough was godfather. The standards of Ramillies were in the same week carried in triumph to the Mansion House and the Duke was fêted as a national hero. But in this year of victory, when Eugene had also won an important battle at Turin and the Allied position was consolidated in Barcelona, were sown the seeds of future mutual Allied distrust. The Dutch were avid for a vast barrier which Marlborough would not concede to them, or else they demanded peace. The Austrians remained content that Marlborough should organize their victories with a minimum of inconvenience to themselves. The alienation of the Queen from Godolphin had begun and Marlborough openly left the Tory party without ever becoming a Whig.

CHAPTER VII

THE WHIGS' SERVANT : 1707

A picture of Marlborough – visit to King of Sweden – fiasco at
   Toulon – ten weeks inactivity in Flanders – Whigs enter
   Cabinet – Harley resigns.

MARLBOROUGH was now at the peak of his military
career. A contemporary Dutchman has drawn
his portrait for us as he then was. At fifty-seven
the " handsome page " had become " a man of
about middle height with the best figure in the
world ; his features without fault, fine sparkling
eyes, good teeth, and his complexion of pink and
white such as the fair sex might envy ; in brief,
except for his legs, which are too thin, one of the
handsomest men ever seen." He spoke agreeably
in bad French, had perfect manners, gentleness,
grace and courage. His faults – boundless ambition and " sordid avarice " – were judged " light
in the scale against the rare gifts of this truly great
man."

When in the previous year Marlborough had
pleaded with his friend Godolphin for one more
year in which to win the war, he little thought that
the year 1707 would prove entirely humiliating to
the Allied cause. Although the striking victory of
Oudenarde was to follow in the next year, the end
of 1706 in fact marked the summit of the Allies'
military success. Had peace been concluded
then, Marlborough would unquestionably have
been deemed the foremost soldier and diplomatist

of his time, possibly of all time. As it was, the campaign of 1707 was based on a serious miscalculation, proved a waste of opportunities and enabled the French to recover from the disasters of the previous year. From the broadest military point of view there was little wrong with Marlborough's plan, which amounted to a double invasion of France. The scheme was that Prince Eugene, with the assistance of the Duke of Savoy's Italians and the German mercenaries dispatched by Marlborough from the north and the British Fleet co-operating from the sea, should lay siege to the important French naval base of Toulon in the Mediterranean. Marlborough calculated that Louis XIV would be compelled to weaken his army in Flanders to meet this danger and then he himself would be able to push into France along the Moselle valley. In his view, this double invasion of France would at once clear the French out of Spain and force Louis to sue for an abject peace. But the French had the advantage of inner lines and were bound to have warning of the attack on Toulon. The Austrians, blind as ever to their long-term interests, were sluggish in moving and from the beginning the time element was against Marlborough. Thus his plan, admirable in theory, was doomed from the start.

Before he opened his own initially defensive campaign in Flanders, Marlborough started on one of those diplomatic missions with strictly limited objectives at which he excelled. He went to visit Charles XII, King of Sweden, who had won a series of resounding victories in northern Europe and then, by turning his arms against

Saxony, had frightened the King of Prussia and the Emperor and distracted their attention from the war against France. While delivering a shower of compliments Marlborough perceived that the young Swedish King, who regarded himself as a Protestant champion, had a "natural aversion" from France and was primarily anxious to crush his particular enemy, Peter the Great, Tsar of Russia. He did not therefore think it necessary to make any precise proposals to divert Charles's eyes from Germany, but simply arranged for the customary bribing of the Swedish Ministers. His judgment proved correct ; by the end of the year Charles XII turned from Central Europe and in due course marched to his destruction at the hands of Peter the Great. After soothing the King of Prussia on his way back to Holland, Marlborough returned to be greeted by the news that two big disasters had already befallen the Allies in the other theatres of war.

On April 25 the Duke of Berwick, the bastard son of James II by Marlborough's sister Arabella, inflicted a considerable defeat on the mixed Allied army at Almanza in Spain, and less than a month later the best French General, Villars, broke through the carefully constructed German defensive lines of Stolhoffen on the Upper Rhine and overran the state of Württemberg. Yet those two defeats need not have upset Marlborough's plans and did not in fact do so. Their main importance was that they unnerved the Dutch and induced them to order their field deputies not to allow Marlborough to attempt any early action in Flanders. And so, as his forces were in any

case markedly inferior to the French, Marlborough sat down to await the result of his
" unique remedy," the attack on Toulon. His
ten weeks' inactivity which now followed was
later harshly criticized. Marlborough himself
asserted in the House of Lords that " it was
impossible to fight the enemy in Flanders till the
detachment was made to cover Toulon." The
Dutch deputies hid their orders to prevent a
battle, in the evident hope that Marlborough
would carry through some manœuvre similar to
the forcing of the lines in 1705 or the bloodless
campaign of 1703 which would enable them to be
" victorious without slaughter." He seems to
have been convinced that he could do nothing
without risking the battle to which he knew the
Dutch were opposed, although, as it happened,
the French General Vendôme, who confronted
him, had also been given orders not to fight. It
is also possible that Marlborough's resentment
at the way in which he had been treated by
the Dutch over the question of the Governor-
Generalship of the Spanish Netherlands in the
previous year decided him to show them that he
would not produce rabbits out of a hat when his
military tricks were so ill-requited.

The Toulon project proved a fiasco. The
Emperor was more concerned to acquire immediate dominions in Italy than to beat the French.
He made a separate treaty whereby the French
troops taken prisoner in Italy were allowed to
return home in exchange for French recognition
of the Emperor's claims in northern Italy, and sent
a large detachment of his troops to Naples,

although Marlborough had begged him not to do so because they were needed at Toulon. Eugene went to Toulon in a completely defeatist mood, and perhaps unavoidable delay enabled the French to bring up reinforcements in good time. After a month the attempt was abandoned. Yet the French voluntarily sank their Toulon fleet and Villars was obliged to retreat across the Rhine partly in consequence of the attempt on Toulon. There is thus good reason to suppose that if the Toulon siege had been persevered with by the Austrians it would have had the vast strategical consequence that Marlborough had foreseen. As it was, even the weakening of the French forces in Flanders, which duly took place as Marlborough had foretold, did not afford him the expected chance of invading France from the north-east. He won Dutch permission for an offensive march, but an aged Dutch cavalry general in charge of the advanced guard, to whom he had given late but written instructions on how to catch the French, lost his way, and afterwards the French withdrew behind the guns of Lille. Marlborough returned to England after this fruitless campaign in a thoroughly bad temper, which was aggravated by political difficulties at home, and the Tory Opposition proceeded to attack the management of the war.

Marlborough's presence was badly needed in England, as differences had arisen between his two partners in the ruling Triumvirate, Godolphin and Harley. It had been with some reluctance that Marlborough had given his support before the campaign began to the movement to

force his son-in-law, the Whig Sunderland, upon
Queen Anne as her second Secretary of State.
The other Secretary of State, Robert Harley, had
seen from the beginning that this was a first step
in the direction of a wholly Whig Administration.
Marlborough himself, though he acquiesced in
Sunderland's appointment, at heart had remained
convinced that a coalition Ministry was the best
instrument with which to win an overwhelming
victory over the French. In August, 1706, he had
written to Godolphin : " I hope the reasonable
men of the other party [the Tories] will not oppose
the enlarging of the bottom so that it may be able
to support itself." This not very elegant phrase
represented his conception of the Whig infiltration as simply a strengthening of the Coalition.
When in England in 1707 he still tried to put this
scheme into effect. He went to his friend the Duke
of Shrewsbury, the leading Whig moderate, at his
house in Oxfordshire and complained to him of
his own and the Queen's uneasiness at the tyranny
of the Whig oligarchy or Junto, as it was called,
and suggested as an alternative to a purely Whig
Ministry a new centre combination which should
include Shrewsbury. But nothing came of this
plan. Consequently Marlborough and Godolphin were obliged to capitulate to the demands of
the Whig Junto, which meant getting rid of
Harley, who intended to stick to the Tories
through thick and thin. But this was not easy,
for the Queen now personally preferred Harley to
Godolphin. It was therefore doubtful whether
she would accept her Treasurer's advice to promote the Whig leaders to office. Marlborough

for a long time hesitated to measure swords with Harley and provoke the Queen. In the course of the summer he told Sarah that he resented his treatment at the hands of the Whigs and particularly their attacks on his brother George at the Admiralty. But he found that if he intended to abide by Godolphin, who managed the war finances so amiably, he had no choice save to yield to the Whigs. A threat was now made by the Whigs to overthrow Godolphin, at the very time that he was completing the Act of Union with Scotland, unless they became supreme in the Cabinet. Harley, seeing which way the wind blew, prepared on his side to offer the Queen an alternative centre government of the very kind that Marlborough had proposed to Shrewsbury. As to the complex manœuvres that followed, it is sufficient to say that Marlborough and Godolphin offered their resignations, which the stubborn Queen was actually willing to accept rather than lose Harley and stomach the Whigs. But Harley, openly opposed by the hitherto victorious Commander-in-Chief, was unable to win the support of the moderate Whigs without whom he could have no majority in the House of Commons and he, not the Queen, finally gave way and resigned. For the next two years a Whig Cabinet, anxious, like Marlborough, for the completest possible victory over France and Spain, ruled England. Marlborough, the ex-Tory, became their servant and the Queen nursed her imaginary grievances and bided her time until she could call Harley back to power.

CHAPTER VIII

A BRIMSTONE OF A WIFE

Sarah's influence on Marlborough – her temper and his patience – parsimony and meanness – a political wife – a case of jealousy.

ANNE's unwillingness to part with Harley was to some extent influenced by the fact that he had an advocate at Court in the Queen's unobtrusive friend and dresser, the red-nosed Abigail Masham, and that by this time Anne had taken Mrs. Masham as her confidante, while her intimate friendship with Sarah Marlborough was a thing of the past. This, however, was a minor factor in the situation, for we have long learned to despise the simple explanation which attributes Marlborough's rise to power in 1702 solely to his wife's friendship with Queen Anne or his ultimate fall in 1711 to Sarah's loss of Anne's affection. Marlborough became the Allied Commander-in-Chief by reason of his own abilities and he lost his position chiefly because he was opposed to making peace when the country wanted peace. Sarah's place in Marlborough's life was different, though equally important. She helped to mould his character as a domineering wife can. He was in fact the henpecked husband *par excellence*. He acquired his monumental patience in the hard school of his own home.

Marlborough had married out of passion inspired by the youth, beauty and vitality of Sarah

Jennings. But in deciding to marry her handsome professional soldier she seems to have been influenced by something more than good looks. One of her few friends, the third Mrs. Burnet, wrote :

> nor was it any blind or unreasonable passion that inclined her to prefer the Duke of Marlborough to all others, though his fortune then was in its infancy, but the effect of judgment. . . . She then saw that good understanding and those excellent qualities that have since made him the wonder of the world.

Sarah's ability to pick out able men is unquestionable. But though her push and thrust may have spurred him on, Marlborough's success was not her work and she damaged rather than sustained his career. For she had a pen steeped in gall and a caustic tongue which lost her more friends than they made. Her temper was fierce and notorious. When a lampoon had compared Marlborough to the Roman Count Belisarius and Sarah asked Bishop Burnet where the comparison lay, he blurted out, truly enough, " he had a brimstone of a wife." She had an infinite capacity for quarrelling which extended not merely to her mother and mother-in-law and to Queen Anne, but to her husband, children, grandchildren and most of her circle of acquaintances. Most of her daughters acquired their mother's temper and the Duke had to pour oil on the troubled family waters. After her husband's death, Sarah used to say that she received obedience and affection only from her three dogs.

Not only was Marlborough's patience home-grown, but so, too, was his parsimony. A detailed study of the relations between Marlborough and his wife would probably show that the reputation which he won in his lifetime for avarice was largely owing to her. From the very beginning she took control of their family finances :

Soon after my marriage [wrote Sarah], when our affairs were so narrow that a good deal of frugality was necessary, Lord Marlborough, though his inclination lay enough that way, yet by reason of an indulgent gentleness that is natural to him he could not manage matters so as was convenient to our circumstances. This obliged me to enter into the management of my family.

Though frugal, the Duke was capable of charity and self-denial. Plenty of examples of his " indulgent gentleness " – gifts to the poor and wounded, loans to St. John and subsidies to the poet Prior, for instance – are to be found. His refusal of the Governor-Generalship of the Netherlands and of Louis XIV's bribes show that power meant more to him than mere money. But Sarah's exaggerated carefulness in money matters was remarkable. She constantly wrote to her husband at the front bothering him about small questions of household management and preferred to waste his time checking a servant's honesty or the contents of the wine cellar than to leave him in peace to fight the war.

Likewise, as we have seen, Sarah constantly pestered her husband about political questions.

Marlborough must be unique in history in having a wife who was for a time virtually his political opponent, a convinced partisan whose views he had to contest by post. From the beginning of the reign Sarah tried to foist the Whig Party on her husband and on the Queen. She wrongly imagined that the Princess Anne would remain her devout political pupil when she became Queen. Inevitably this alienated a ruler who was fully conscious of the dignity of her office. Moreover, Sarah came to neglect Anne, stayed away from Court for long spells, interrupted her conversation, interfered in her personal affairs. It was not surprising that Anne turned for comfort elsewhere, and when after a long and violent quarrel Sarah was indiscreet enough to make some rude remarks about Anne's husband, Prince George, Sarah's loss of office as well as influence could only be a question of time.

In 1704, at the age of forty-four, Sarah came to the conclusion that her husband was unfaithful. The loss of her only son and the knowledge that she could not expect another may excuse or explain the accusations which she then made, naming a specific person. Marlborough assured her that he " never sent to this woman," although he added, " as I know your temper I am very sensible that what I say signifies nothing." On the eve of his march to the Danube he pleaded with her :

> If the thought of the children that we have had, or aught else that has ever been dear between us, can oblige you to be so good

natured as not to leave my bed for the remaining time, I shall take it kindly to my dying day, and do most faithfully promise you that I will take the first occasion of leaving England, and assure you that you may rest quiet that from that time you shall never more be troubled with my hated sight.

When she saw him off at Harwich she handed him a " paper " evidently containing further recriminations. " I do own to you," he wrote in reply, " I have had more melancholy thoughts and spleen at what you said in that paper than I am able to express." But a little later she relented and forgave. She even offered to go with him on the march to the Danube and he was able to take the Harwich " paper " out of his strong box and burn it. Who shall say that this quarrel is the only example of Sarah's cruelty to her husband or that this was the only suspicion that he aroused ? Six years later old Lady Wentworth went to church and afterwards described how –

in the next pew to me there sits a young lady very genteel and very fair, but I think far from a beauty, but it is said she is kept by the Duke of Marlborough . . .

Perhaps it was but village scandal. But who would have blamed the Duke if patient, henpecked, troubled by a thousand personal and public cares, he had turned for a while from his abnormal termagant wife and sought comfort elsewhere ?

CHAPTER IX

Queen Anne and the Whigs – general election – loss of Ghent
and Bruges – battle of Oudenarde – siege of Lille.

AFTER the dismissal of Harley at the behest of
the Whig oligarchy, Marlborough and Godolphin,
formerly Tories and then non-party men, became
the prisoners of the Whigs. Under the inexorable
pressure of the parliamentary facts they had surrendered. Queen Anne was as stubborn as ever.
She refused to be more than polite to her new
Cabinet Ministers and did not hide her distaste
for some of the leading members of her Government – with one exception, her Commander-in-
Chief. Sarah, seeing the Queen's antagonism to
the Whigs and notably to her son-in-law, Sunderland, wrote Anne abusive letters. Godolphin
was aware that the Queen would dismiss him as
soon as she dared. Both therefore appealed to
Marlborough to pacify the Queen, and when he
was in the midst of the 1708 campaign he had to
employ his time writing soothingly to Anne, trying to keep the Home Government in being while
he won the war. But gone was the intimacy of
the early days. Frequent threats of resignation
were uttered both by him and by Godolphin,
but Marlborough's threats were mostly bluffs.
The tactless conduct of Sarah, the growing bore-
dom of Godolphin, who declared his life was a
burden, the high-handed blackmail of the Whigs,

the intrigues of the dismissed Harley, the in-
difference of the Queen never turned him from
his determination to see the war through. Time,
he was convinced, was all he needed. Once
more, he pleaded, " Give me one more year."

A General Election was now due and a not
unexpected event played into the hands of the
Whigs. Louis XIV gave permission for a small
expedition to invade Scotland in the name of the
Pretender, " James III." Scottish discontent with
the immediate results of the Act of Union, passed
in the previous year, offered an opportunity ;
the genius of Admiral Forbin, commander of the
Dunkirk privateers, provided the means. But
Forbin's half-hearted expedition, carrying a pack
of sea-sick exiles, was defeated as much by the
elements as by Marlborough's elaborate precau-
tions, and not a soldier landed. Nevertheless
panic was widespread. The Whigs, who dubbed
all Tories Jacobites – that is, secret followers of
the exiled Stuarts – were given an election cry
against " traitors " and the Queen's hopes that
the moderate Tories would still hold the balance
in Parliament were disappointed. The Whigs
duly gained their majority and pressed for fuller
representation in the Cabinet, demanding the
Presidency of the Council for their chief, Lord
Somers. The Queen resisted and Marlborough
was begged to come back from Flanders to use
his influence in the Whig favour. He not un-
naturally refused ; he wrote her letters as he was
asked to do, but he knew that they would be of
no effect ; and he plunged into his plans for the
campaign, fearful lest the notorious political

difficulties in London should induce the Dutch, now tiring of the war, to rupture the alliance.

Marlborough aimed at achieving success in the new campaign by the use of surprise. He arranged that three armies should take the field in the northern theatre. The Imperialist general, the Elector of Hanover, the future King George I of England, was to operate with 45,000 men on the Rhine; Prince Eugene was to have 40,000 men on the Moselle; and Marlborough himself was to have 80,000 men in Flanders. He did not expect the Elector to act other than defensively, but he secretly planned that Eugene's army should join his and crush the French, who had about 90,000 men under the lascivious but not incompetent Marshal Vendôme. After a visit to Hanover to persuade the Elector to co-operate, Marlborough took up his headquarters with the army and awaited Eugene's arrival. On June 11 he wrote to Eugene, " I request you to hasten in all diligence, for we can only reckon on a surprise which will depend on the little time you may take for your march between the Moselle and the Meuse." But the customary delays of the Austrian and other German troops prevented Eugene from setting out and meanwhile the French had prepared their own surprise blow. The discontent of the Belgians with the Dutch administration in the conquered Spanish provinces was exploited. A bold march by Vendôme across Marlborough's flank enabled the French to retake Ghent and Bruges at the beginning of July and to threaten Marlborough's communications with Ostend. For once Marlborough appears to have been caught by surprise, since the French had feinted against Louvain while he had hesitated to uncover Brussels.

Thus when Eugene at last arrived, but without his troops, to join the Duke in his camp near Brussels, he found him sunk in despondency. Physical weakness was the consequence or the accompaniment of mental depression. He was laid low with fever and had to be bled. But the presence of Eugene invigorated him. He decided no longer to await Eugene's dilatory army to give him a decisive advantage in man power, but to make an immediate counter-stroke. Vendôme, after he had taken Bruges and Ghent, determined to lay siege to Oudenarde, a small town which commanded the Scheldt between Ghent and Tournai on the French frontier. Marlborough took advantage of this move to persuade the French into believing that he was now advancing on the Scheldt merely in order to prevent the siege of Oudenarde, but in reality he was coming at them with battle in mind. When Cadogan with the advanced guard occupied the village of Lessines to the right of the Scheldt the deception had worked, for the French had no expectation of an Allied offensive and decided to cross the Scheldt lower down with a view to marching on Menin, another key fortress in Allied hands. At 1 a.m. on the morning of July 11 Cadogan crossed the Scheldt south of Oudenarde with sixteen battalions and eight squadrons and ran into the French advanced guard consisting of seven Swiss battalions and twelve squadrons. As soon as the heads of the main army began to cross the pontoons which he had placed across the river, Cadogan decided to attack ; the Swiss battalions were thrust back and surrendered and the French cavalry were driven off. Vendôme could at first scarcely credit the arrival of the Allied army, whose infantry had marched fifty miles in sixty hours, but he decided to crush Cadogan with all his force. Trusting to his left wing simultaneously to launch an attack, he himself took command on the right. The left, through a misunderstanding, failed him.

Whether Cadogan's original attack was made on Marlborough's orders is uncertain. But as soon as the Duke took command the clash of advanced guards was developed by him into an " encounter battle," each regiment falling into its place to broaden the firing line as it reached the field across the river. Cadogan's forces became part of the right of the battle line and at six o'clock in the evening Eugene was put in command of the whole of the Allied right. On the left an essentially infantry battle in ground enclosed by woods and rivulets developed and ultimately, by bringing up his Dutch troops on the extreme left of his line, Marlborough threatened to envelop the French right flank completely. Although Eugene with the British cavalry more than held his own in the open ground on the right, it was on the Allied left that the battle was won. Indeed, the French left, because it did not take its full share in the fighting, escaped relatively unharmed. But the whole French army was saved from annihilation only by the dark. It lost some 15,000 men in casualties and prisoners against the Allies' 3,000.

G M

At Oudenarde Marlborough showed his genius
for a type of contest entirely different from
Blenheim or Ramillies. He thrust his men into
line at the crucial points and shifted his troops
from left to right with consummate coolness of
judgment. But he owed much to the enemy's
mistakes. Contrary to all the canons of war, he
had been able to cross a river in face of a superior
enemy late in the afternoon after a long and tiring
march and by means of surprise win an overwhelming victory.

When the battle of Oudenarde took place the
two armies were facing the wrong way ; the
Allies looked towards Holland, the French towards France. Afterwards the Allies were at last
over the French frontier, while the French, by
withdrawing towards Ghent, threatened the communications between the Allied camp and the sea.
Marlborough now proposed a daring project to
Eugene, whose own troops had just joined him
to give them a united force of 100,000 men. Let
them mask the French frontier fortresses and advance into the heart of France. If they did so,
the French would be obliged to leave Ghent and
follow them. But the plan was too bold for
Eugene. So instead, Marlborough vainly tried to
move Vendôme from Ghent by ravaging the
French provinces of Artois and Picardy. The
Allies then laid siege to Lille, the biggest of the
French frontier fortresses and one of the largest
towns in France. The French command of the
Bruges-Ghent canal made the obtaining of supplies for the siege through Ostend a matter of
great difficulty. However, convoys were brought

through and on August 13, the anniversary of
Blenheim, Lille was invested ; Eugene took
charge of the siege while Marlborough directed
the covering army, much inferior in numbers to
the French who had more than replaced their
heavy losses at Oudenarde since the Duke of
Berwick, previously stationed on the Meuse, had
now joined Vendôme with 27,000 men. So confident was Marlborough once again in the moral
superiority of his men that he would have been
glad to fight another battle ; but the French
twice refused it. Meanwhile, the siege of Lille,
which was defended by the gallant old Marshal
Boufflers with 16,000 men, went badly for the
Allies. When in September Eugene was wounded
and Marlborough for a time took over the operations he found grave deficiencies in supplies and
incompetence among the engineers responsible
for the sapping. Supplies were further endan-
gered by the French occupying the line of
the Scheldt and cutting communications with
Brussels and Holland. But the road to the sea
remained open and seven days later the French
effort to relieve the town, not by fighting a battle
but by stopping the Allied convoys, was finally
defeated at the engagement of Wynendael, when
General Webb with 6,000 men repulsed a much
superior force—a feat for which Marlborough
gave him full credit, in spite of Thackeray's story
in *Esmond*. On October 22 Lille surrendered
after ten weeks siege, and at the price of some
12,000 casualties to the besiegers, though the
citadel still resisted. It was not Boufflers' fault,
and it is to his honour that by his courageous

defence he prevented an imminent threat of his
country being overrun by invaders. For if Lille
had fallen as quickly as Marlborough had hoped
it had still been his intention to thrust into the
heart of France during that campaign. Instead,
the Duke perforce turned to recapture Ghent and
Bruges. He first forced the Scheldt at four
separate points. Vendôme's counter-move in
laying siege to Brussels, which had long been
exposed to attack, was a failure and by the beginning of 1709 Brussels was relieved and Ghent
and Bruges fell to the Allies. Thus the campaign,
which contrary to the accepted rules lasted into
the depths of winter, concluded according to
Marlborough's " heart's desire."

CHAPTER X

THE THIRD MARLBOROUGH

The three Marlboroughs — secret correspondence with Berwick —
its motives — relations with Jacobites — their four phases.

THERE were three Marlboroughs. First, there
was the public figure, the patient, courteous,
inscrutable, ever victorious "Milord." Secondly,
there was the harassed and henpecked private
man, subject to vast fits of depression and actual
physical illness when things did not go right —
the man who appealed, cajoled and threatened,
and abused his enemies in his private correspondence. Thirdly, there was the master in-
triguer who held secret conclaves with French or
Jacobite agents, penned anonymous letters and
spun meaningless phrases of good advice merely
in order to safeguard his own personal position
and property in the event of counter-
revolution.

Never in the whole of Marlborough's life are
his three selves more fully visible in the light of
history than during the year 1708. This was
one of the most glorious years in his military
career. Yet during the same season the Duke
not only had that tremendous fit of depression
at the beginning of the campaign, but was reduced to a constant state of worry by the stream
of complaining letters which reached him from
London. He knew that since the Whig

infiltration into the Ministry Godolphin had lost the confidence of the Queen, that she had resented being forced to admit more Whigs into the Cabinet and that the Government was maintained in power almost solely by his own victories. Finally, simply by way of precaution, without saying a word to a soul, Marlborough after Oudenarde entered into a secret and indirect correspondence with the Ministers of Louis XIV to discover the likelihood of peace negotiations.

This secret correspondence was carried on through Marlborough's nephew, the Duke of Berwick. Berwick had become by dint of sheer skill one of the leading generals in the French Army, but he remained loyal to the exiled Court of St. Germains, and did what he could to promote the claims of his half-brother, the Old Pretender, " James III," to the throne of Great Britain. Marlborough's correspondence with the exiled Court was not, of course, a new departure ; but now it took a novel turn. As there are gaps in the surviving letters, the details are a little obscure, but it seems that Berwick wrote first to thank his uncle for exerting his influence to obtain mercy for Lord Griffin, an aged Jacobite who had been captured from a French ship during the abortive expedition of the early spring. At the same time Berwick suggested a personal meeting between them to discuss possible terms of peace, but Marlborough evaded so compromising a step. As the correspondence developed, Marlborough expressed his wish that the French should make some peace proposals publicly in Holland. He did not specify exactly what proposals might prove acceptable but said they must " conform to the interests of my country." Although the correspondence continued by fits and starts, nothing came of it, because the French said that it was against the dignity of Louis XIV to open negotiations in Holland and demanded an armistice first. Two points, however, emerge from this section of the Marlborough-Berwick secret correspondence. First, Marlborough was committing himself to nothing dishonourable. His motive was to ensure that if peace negotiations were opened he should be kept informed about them and not presented with an accomplished fact by the French and Dutch. Yet, secondly, it was typical of the man that Marlborough also hoped to get something for himself if by any unexpected chance peace negotiations should prove fruitful, for in one letter he took care to remind Berwick that three years earlier an agent of the French King had promised him 2,000,000 livres (about £300,000) if peace were concluded with his help.

Another section of this same correspondence well defines Marlborough's real attitude to the Pretender. He told Berwick that he was willing to serve the Pretender " without prejudice to the interests of my country " and provided that in promoting the Pretender's interests he was not merely benefiting France. Moreover, he clearly stated that he could not help the Pretender unless he were " recalled by the nation." Since " James III " was as firm a Roman Catholic as his father and a notorious pensioner of France, the likelihood of his recall was small. Thus all that Marlborough did was to inform the exiled Court that if after the death of Queen Anne England expressed a unanimous wish to bring back the Stuarts (instead, according to the Act of Settlement, of bringing in the Electoral family of Hanover), he personally would not stand in their way. By this pledge he hoped to safeguard his own position and ward off a justly merited revenge for the manner in which he had treated the unfortunate James II.

This policy of "reinsuring" himself against the event of a Jacobite Restoration was probably the dominant motive for Marlborough's prolonged secret contacts with the exiled Stuarts. But there were other motives and in his thirty-year maintenance of these contacts it is possible to detect four distinct phases. The first phase was during the reign of William III, when Marlborough headed a sort of inchoate opposition to William and his Dutch favourites. He then thought that it would do no harm to bring the English Jacobites into his hotch-potch coalition against the unpopular Dutch ruler. But when in 1701 William selected Marlborough to carry on his feud with France the Jacobite connections were at once loosened. Although Marlborough continued to inform the Jacobite agents that "in the proper time and place he will pay his debt to King James," there was reported in St. Germains to be "a manifest cooling" on Marlborough's part, and it was even proposed that the Pretender should marry one of his daughters in order presumably to warm him up again. Berwick himself never seems to have seriously believed that Marlborough meant much by his polite messages to St. Germains, but he kept on writing to his uncle in case one day the correspondence might prove a useful channel of communication. By the middle of the war most of the other leading Jacobites came to agree with Berwick that Marlborough's professions of friendship meant nothing.

Thus we come to 1708–9, and the third phase in Marlborough's relations with the Jacobites, in which he made use of his special position to open a window onto the diplomatic schemes of the Court of Versailles. Ever since the Allies overran Belgium and the frontier of Holland was made safe, Marlborough was gnawed by the fear that the Dutch would desert the Grand Alliance and thereby put an end to the war. His oft avowed desire for peace was only for peace on the most stringent terms. Consequently he hoped by his letters to Berwick to prevent any separate negotiation which might cut the ground from under the British Government's feet.

The fourth phase of Marlborough's relations with the Jacobites followed his own fall from power in 1711. He then came to have two objects in view. First, there was again, and slightly more urgently, his policy of personal reinsurance. Marlborough hoped and expected that when Queen Anne died the Hanoverians would peacefully ascend the throne. But there was just an outside chance that if the Pretender should change his religion the Stuarts would be brought back instead. In the late autumn of 1713 Marlborough sent a messenger or spy to

Paris to see how the land lay. But he then had a
second object. By this time the Treaty of Utrecht
had been signed and the Tories were in full cry
against the Whig " warmongers." Marlborough
was afraid that in this revengeful mood they
might confiscate his estates and he begged
Louis XIV – his arch-enemy ! – to intercede with
Queen Anne – his former friend ! – to see that
Parliament did not beggar him. In all the
fantasy of Marlborough's elaborate but hollow
intrigues with the Court of St. Germains nothing
is more extraordinary than this episode. At
that time too he, the notorious miser, even thought
it worth while to send " a small sum " to Queen
Mary of Modena as an earnest of his good faith.
At precisely that moment, however, the Duke
was also assuring the Elector of Hanover by post
that his friends in England were anxious to serve
the Hanoverian cause and that he would do
everything in his power to prevent the Tory
Government from bringing in the Pretender.
Thus he put a small sum on both the competitors
for the throne of England and, having insured
himself both ways, was on the death of Queen
Anne restored to his estates and offices without
difficulty.

But still the comedy dragged on. As late as
1716 an eminent Jacobite reported that Marlborough had told a Jacobite agent " with tears
in his eyes " that he intended " to serve James
III." But the Duke of Berwick summed up the
true state of the matter when he wrote in this
same year that –

Marlborough had for these many years been in correspondence with his nephew [himself] and has always given assurances of his zeal for King James but to this hour he has never explained in what manner he intended it.

CHAPTER XI

THE TWICE-LOST PEACE: 1709 – 1710

The Dutch Barrier Treaty – peace negotiations with France –
the Allied " preliminaries " – battle of Malplaquet – fall of
Tournai and Mons – request for captain-generalship for life –
quarrel with Queen over Abigail Masham – peace negotiations at Gertruydenberg.

MARLBOROUGH'S successes in the campaign of
1708, combined with French and Spanish defeats
in other war theatres and a terrible frost which
ruined the French crops and threatened starvation,
made Louis XIV extremely desirous of peace.
Informal contacts had long been maintained
between France and Holland with a view to
seizing any favourable opportunity for negotiations. The Dutch were now offered territorial
concessions by France. Simultaneously, the Whig
Ministry in London became anxious to obtain
Dutch support for the Protestant succession to
Queen Anne and for the continuance of the war
until the wealth of the Spanish Empire was at
their disposal. Thus the Whig Ministers now
spontaneously renewed the proposal that in return
for a guarantee of the succession Great Britain
should secure for the Dutch their coveted barrier
of fortresses in the Spanish Netherlands. Marlborough, however, strongly opposed conceding
the Dutch their barrier before a general peace
was concluded. His dominant idea was to keep
the Grand Alliance together. If the Dutch were
granted special conditions he thought the Austrians would be alienated and that the Dutch,

secure in their treaty, would at once become less enthusiastic for the continuation of the war. But, as so often, a personal element entered into his calculations. He had not abandoned the hope that he would one day when the war was over become Governor-General of the Spanish Netherlands. The Emperor had recently renewed this offer. If those Netherlands, however, were to be partitioned with British agreement in order to give the Dutch their barrier fortresses, the Emperor would certainly not be so willing to confer their governorship on a British general. Hence, by deliberate procrastination and intrigue, he did his utmost to rupture the Barrier negotiations.

Marlborough had no such secret motive for preventing the success of the negotiations with France, but he naturally objected to any separate Franco-Dutch discussions until the Allies had agreed together on demands that could be jointly presented to the French delegates. He succeeded in shelving the Barrier negotiations and inducing the Dutch and Austrians to agree on a joint ultimatum to France which was euphemistically called the " preliminaries." By these France was to surrender the entire Spanish Empire, consisting of the Netherlands, Spain itself, the Indies, Naples, Sicily and Milan, as well as Strasbourg and Alsace, to the Habsburg Emperor and to yield a group of fortresses to the Dutch. In the event of Louis XIV's grandson, Philip of Anjou, refusing to evacuate Spain within two months, the Allies were by Article XXXVII to keep their gains and renew the war. Torcy, the French

Foreign Minister, who came to Holland to treat, gave way point by point on all these severe terms, but finally refused to sign the Treaty without reference to Versailles. Confident that the French were beaten beyond recovery, Marlborough fully expected the French King would be compelled to sign and looked forward cheerfully to peace. But Louis could not agree to the clauses which in effect obliged him to make immediate war on his own grandson, and the Allies' ultimatum was rejected.

Marlborough was staggered by the news. "Are there then no counter-proposals ? " he inquired. He thought, however, that if the Dutch were firm the French would be compelled to comply. Negotiations continued for a time, the Allies suggesting as an alternative to the obnoxious Article XXXVII that Louis XIV should hand over to them three towns in Spain as well as three in Flanders as a guarantee for the evacuation of Spain. But to force the Spaniards to surrender three towns was as hard as making them drive their own choice as King from his throne, and thus the war had to go on.

There is no question that the British Government was mainly responsible for the failure of the peace negotiations at a time when Marlborough's victories had forced France so low that she would have conceded nearly anything. Although some play has recently been made with an isolated quotation from Torcy's *Mémoires*, there is no evidence to show that Marlborough had any serious doubts about Article XXXVII until after the " preliminaries " were rejected. Then both he and Eugene laid the blame for the breakdown of negotiations on the Dutch, which was entirely unfair. For the Dutch were only acting as the mouthpieces of the Allies and consented to the far-reaching character of the " preliminaries " only out of deference to the British Whig Government and in the hope of thereby obtaining a guarantee of their Barrier. Marlborough became equally critical of the demand for the three Spanish towns and thought that the better plan would be for the Allies to make a separate treaty with the French, which would prevent them " playing tricks," and then themselves concentrate their war efforts against Spain. He optimistically thought that they could drive Philip out of Spain in six months if his grandfather ceased to help him.

Marlborough's attitude to the diplomatic negotiations of 1709 therefore differed from that of the Government of which he was a leading member. He differed from the Whigs over their desire to conclude a Barrier Treaty with the Dutch, and neglected his instructions on this point ; he differed from them in his belief that if the Dutch were once guaranteed their Barrier, they would immediately desert the Grand Alliance ; and he differed from them as to the best method of driving Philip of Anjou from Spain. At the same time he had become so accustomed to deferring to other people that whatever confidential views he might express he never exerted himself to enforce his own point of view on his own Government. Thus it was by sins of omission rather than of commission that Marlborough helped to prolong

the war in 1709. He was still hopeful that the
French were so demoralized that one more battle
would bring them to their knees. This was
the mood in which at the beginning of June he
entered upon the campaign.

Not only the unsuccessful peace negotiations,
but a combination of other circumstances, delayed
the opening of the campaign of 1709. The frosty
winter had been followed by a cold spring which
restricted the forage. Heavy rains washed away
the roads. The previous campaign had continued
unusually late and a respite of six months was
needed to collect new mercenaries. Had Marlborough been able to start sooner, there were no
opposing forces to prevent a march deep into the
heart of France. As it was, in spite of the starvation which stalked his land, the Great Monarch,
his glory now tarnished, had been able to rally
the French people. Villars, the only French
general whose career is comparable with that of
Marlborough or Eugene, had been put in command and by dint of push and bluff had gathered
an army of a sort behind him. He was able to
use it to man the defences which he constructed
to the west of the line of frontier fortresses. Lille
had fallen, but there still remained three powerfully fortified towns – Ypres, Tournai and Mons.
Marlborough decided against the hazard of
attacking the gaunt but grim and determined
French army which held these new lines of La
Bassée south-west of Lille. Instead, after feinting
against Ypres, he laid siege to the town of Tournai,
which, after much deep sapping to avoid the mines,

was surrendered by the Governor on July 30.

After the fall of Tournai the Allied army moved against Mons, still further away from the main road to Paris, and Villars, surprised by their decision, left his own lines with a view to interrupting the siege. Between the two armies there ran a screen of forest, but in the forest were two big gaps. The Allies reached the northern gap first, but Villars was first at the southern gap – known as the gap of Malplaquet. Both sides were prepared to fight. According to one opinion Marlborough tempted Villars by leaving the gaps open. Another opinion has it that Villars surprised Marlborough by feinting at the northern gap before occupying the southern. In any case there seems little doubt that Villars was willing, and had permission from Versailles, to try a defensive battle in order to strengthen the morale of the raw French troops and that, on the other side, Marlborough and Eugene preferred an attempt to destroy the last French army rather than simply cover the siege of Mons. Villars occupied the woods on both sides of the Malplaquet gap with infantry, built redans (earthworks) in his centre and drew up his troops in a concave V-shape so that if the enemy entered between the two receding wings they would be overwhelmed by a withering fire. But the experienced generals opposite were too wise to fall into so obvious a trap. Their plan, on the contrary, was to assault the two French wings so fiercely that Villars would be obliged to weaken his centre ; then fifteen battalions of British infantry, kept in reserve, could break through.

Hm

The battle was delayed for a day while the Allies awaited the arrival of eighteen squadrons under General Withers that were coming from Tournai. Marlborough was willing to begin without them, but Eugene refused and it seems that he was right. For, although the extra day enabled Villars to fortify further his formidable position, Withers' men were to play a decisive part.

The battle opened on September 11, as planned, with a fierce attack on the French wings resting on or in the woods. The resistance was unexpectedly severe. On the left wing of the Allies the splendid Dutch Blue Guards were mown down. On the right, commanded by Prince Eugene, the Germans were at first successful, but then checked. Marlborough had personally to go up and call a halt to prevent the annihilation of the Dutch on the left. Some blamed the young Dutch prince who had bravely led the charge for going beyond his orders and making a reality of an attack which was only intended as a feint. There was no basis for this. Both French wings had to be assaulted simultaneously. But the battle was decided on the right largely by the arrival of Withers' men, who entered the woods at the extreme north by an unguarded path and threatened to outflank the whole French position. Villars denuded his centre to meet the threat and a desperate and bloody struggle swayed to and fro on the western edge of the woods. The redans were left almost defenceless and the British infantry was able to clear the way for a cavalry advance and the French line split asunder. Villars was badly wounded just as he heard this news and was preparing a counter-stroke. Marshal Boufflers, who took over the command, organized six vain charges against the British infantry who had occupied the deserted earthworks in the centre. He then withdrew his men in good order from the battlefield and the Allies were too exhausted to pursue.

Judged by the larger issues, Malplaquet was a French victory. It is true that the French were forced to evacuate the field and abandon Mons to its fate. But with inferior troops both in numbers and in quality (the French were about 80,000 and the Allies 100,000) they had inflicted far larger casualties. The Allies lost nearly one-fifth of their men, the French about 11,000. Marlborough himself had to confess it was " a very murdering battle." Moreover, by entrenching himself and awaiting the onslaught Villars could scarcely have hoped for a decisive victory. What he had done was to restore the honour of the French Army, to keep his forces together and to stave off the invasion of France. When Marlborough wrote home after the battle, " God Almighty be praised, it is now in our power to have what peace we please," he was deceiving himself. Malplaquet raised the spirits of the French. Never again in the war was there to be so fine an opportunity of a Carthaginian peace as was thrown away after the Oudenarde campaign.

The citadel of Tournai had at length fallen on September 3 and Mons fell on October 25. But in Spain there were no corresponding Allied successes, even though Louis XIV had been compelled to withdraw most of his troops from the

Peninsula. Philip of Anjou controlled most of
Spain except Catalonia and thus the parrot cry of
" No peace without Spain," which Marlborough
and Godolphin had originated and which had now
been wholeheartedly adopted by the Whig Government, was nowhere nearer realization. But
the nation, after eight weary and costly years of
war, was demanding peace. Swimming with the
current, Queen Anne could prepare her revenge
on the Whigs whom she detested.

While Marlborough had been fighting Malplaquet, Lord Townshend, the Whig statesman who
had been sent from London as his diplomatic
colleague, continued to negotiate with the Dutch
about their Barrier Treaty. His view and that of
the Home Government was that if the Dutch were
once promised their Barrier they would be bound
to continue the war until the French agreed to
surrender the " cautionary towns " in Spain and
thereby pave the way for expelling the French
prince from Madrid. Marlborough, who followed
the negotiations closely, disagreed utterly. He
still favoured a separate treaty between the Allies
and France and a war against Spain alone con-
ducted by himself. As to the Barrier Treaty, he
adhered to his opinion that once it was signed the
Dutch would desert the Alliance. He also thought
the Dutch demands excessive (as he privately
explained to his Austrian friends) and that the
Treaty should not be signed without a specific
promise from the Dutch not to make peace until
the entire Spanish Empire was surrendered by
Philip of Anjou. He therefore washed his hands

of both affairs and left Townshend to sign in
October, 1709, a Barrier Treaty whereby the
Dutch were promised a long line of fortresses in
return simply for a guarantee of the Hanoverian
succession to the British throne. But the subse-
quent conduct of the Dutch proved that
Marlborough was entirely wrong in his fore-
bodings.

His refusal to take part in these diplomatic
negotiations was the first outward sign of his
declining influence. The Whig Junto had taken
over the real direction of foreign policy and
domestic questions. Throughout the summer, for
instance, they had insisted that Lord Orford, their
last member without office, should be put at the
head of the Admiralty. Marlborough and
Godolphin grumbled and Queen Anne openly
objected. But Marlborough gave way. The
Queen, every inch a Stuart, proved less willing to
consent to the arrogant Whig dominance and she
secretly consulted Harley, the Tory leader, who
came up the back stairs to see her through the
connivance of Abigail Masham.

Abigail's growing influence not only worried
the Whigs, but excited the jealousy of Sarah Marlborough, who, though she had long ceased to be
friendly with her Sovereign, was still her First
Lady-in-Waiting. Sarah's quarrels with the
Queen and his friend Godolphin's subjection to
the Whigs made Marlborough all the more conscious of his declining power. He tried to
rehabilitate himself in the eyes of the foreign
Courts and generals by asking the Queen in
October, 1709, to make him Captain-General for

life, an unprecedented request which she unhesitatingly refused. On her refusal he wrote her a reproachful letter. The result of the transaction was to weaken his influence with the Queen and to give a handle to his Tory enemies, who accused him of aspiring to a Cromwellian dictatorship.

A further cause of dissension arose between Marlborough and Queen Anne after his return from the war in the following month. Anne proposed to appoint Abigail's brother, Colonel Hill, to a vacant regiment. Marlborough strongly objected and again threatened to resign. He proposed to his Cabinet colleagues that they should jointly demand Abigail's dismissal and that he should confront the Queen with the alternative of dismissing either Abigail or himself. The Queen realized that she had gone too far and agreed to withdraw the Hill appointment; but she clung to Abigail. Marlborough still wanted to fight, but was overborne by Godolphin and the more timorous members of the Cabinet. In their view it was a bad issue on which to attack the Queen. Marlborough therefore withdrew his resignation, stomached Abigail and merely wrote pathetically to Anne complaining that his " love, zeal and duty " had " not been able to protect me against the malice of a Bedchamber Woman."

In March, 1710, leaving all this distasteful intrigue behind him, Marlborough went back to The Hague to prepare for the next campaign. But first he had to keep a watchful eye upon some new peace negotiations in progress in Holland at what was known as the Congress of Gertruydenberg. Louis XIV had not been especially cheered by the battle of Malplaquet and his delegates again offered the Allies good terms. He would give up Alsace to the Emperor and pay a subsidy to the Allies to help them dethrone his grandson. But the Dutch, who acted as the Allied spokesmen, stuck to the harsh demand that Louis himself should expel his grandson from Spain within two months. If he failed to do this, the Allies were to be free to renew the war and to keep the " cautionary towns " which Louis was expected to yield in order to gain even two months' grace. In making these excessive demands the Dutch were, however, only the catspaws of the Whigs, to whom they were now bound hand and foot by the Barrier Treaty. From Marlborough's private letters to Godolphin we know that the Dutch would have been perfectly willing to let Philip of Anjou have the throne of Sicily, which belonged to the Spanish Empire, to induce him to leave Spain quietly. The Austrians for their part would not hear of Sicily, but would have been ready to waive the demand that Louis should drive his grandson from Spain if the " cautionary towns " were surrendered. The British Whigs alone stood by the full rigour of the demands. Marlborough, who had decided to abandon diplomacy and to confine himself to military activity, played no effective part at all in this vital matter. Indeed, he had resigned himself to a philosophic contemplation of political events and described changing the views of the Dutch or of the Queen as " painting a blackamoor white." So he stood idly by and watched the last chance of a triumphant peace being dissipated.

CHAPTER XII

WAR WITHOUT END: 1710-1711

Reaction in favour of Tories – Shrewsbury enters Cabinet – campaign of 1710 – Godolphin dismissed – Marlborough humiliated – Sarah dismissed – death of Emperor Leopold – Ne Plus Ultra lines crossed – siege of Bouchain – war weariness.

AFTER Oudenarde Queen Anne exclaimed, " Oh, Lord, when will all this dreadful bloodshed cease ? " After Malplaquet she began to conclude that it was her duty to take positive steps to end the war. She reflected much articulate and inarticulate public opinion which was steadily veering against Godolphin and the Whig Administration. In consequence of the apparently unending war, food prices were rising, taxation was heavy and the methods of recruiting severe. The supporters of war to the finish and of peace at a moderate price had become divided on distinct class lines. On the one hand, the commercial classes, in search of the reputed riches of the Spanish Empire, were pretty solidly behind the Whigs, and the new Bank of England continued to put its money on " no peace without Spain." On the other hand, the landed proprietors were sickened by the large increases in the land tax. As Sir John Packington was to put it a year later, only an end to the war would " prevent the beggaring of the nation and prevent the moneyed men becoming lords of us who have lands."

On top of social and economic discontents came

a political dispute. On November 5, the day on
which William III had landed at Tor Bay, a
High Church parson, Dr. Henry Sacheverell,
preached a sermon in St. Paul's Cathedral con-
demning the doctrines of the Glorious Revolution. This infuriated the Whig Government,
while Godolphin, whose Whiggism was scarcely
noticeable, was offended at what he thought to
be a personal attack on himself in the sermon.
So the decision was taken to impeach Sacheverell
for high treason. He was condemned in the
House of Lords by a few votes, but received a
purely nominal punishment. The effect of im-
peaching a somewhat obscure clergyman for a
sermon was disastrous for the Whigs. The
Opposition Tories were able to raise their old
battle-cry, " The Church in danger ! " – an
alarm to which even Marlborough's own chaplain
succumbed. Property owners were also concerned at the subversive republican ideas which
they detected in the terms of the impeachment.
From this time onwards it became obvious that
a General Election would mean the defeat of the
Government, and Queen Anne, now out of sym-
pathy with the Marlboroughs, discarded cronies
of her younger days, joyfully awaited the Whigs'
overthrow.

Taking advantage of the Government's de-
moralization, Harley, the Queen's secret Tory
adviser, began to detach the weaker members of
the Cabinet from their loyalty to the Whig Junto
and to Godolphin. He held out to them promises
of high office in a reconstructed Cabinet and
first preference shares in the Queen's favour.

Such was the atmosphere of intrigue and Royal antagonism which Marlborough discovered in London in the winter of 1709 and was to be the background of his next campaign. On April 15, after he had sailed, Queen Anne, without consulting Godolphin, nominally her chief Minister, introduced the Duke of Shrewsbury into the Cabinet as Lord Chamberlain. This was the thin end of the wedge. Shrewsbury was a Whig by repute and he and Marlborough had been friends for many years, but Marlborough knew at once that he was brought in as Harley's Trojan horse. Thenceforward, throughout spring and summer, Marlborough saw gloomily but helplessly the doom opening for his friends and supporters in England. He faced the prospect with patient resignation. He hoped that a General Election would be postponed for the time being, so that the Whig majority in the Commons, still eager for the war, would be preserved ; and even for a time imagined that some lucky turn in the campaign would revive his personal credit with his sovereign. " If we have a battle," he wrote in May, " it must be the last. . . . I hope God will bless me with another opportunity of giving a mark of my zeal for the Queen and my country, and then I shall be less concerned at the behaviour [sic] I have received of late."

But there was to be no " last battle." Flanders had become the major theatre of war and the French had concentrated the bulk of their manpower under the now recovered Villars to resist the Allied penetration into France. Before Villars

took up his command, however, Marlborough
and Eugene made their first move early in the
season by turning the French lines and laying
siege to Douai, the capture of which would open
the way for direct invasion of France. But this
town, well fortified and defended, did not in
fact fall until June 26, two months later. In
the course of the siege Marlborough had an
opportunity to attack the French Army which
he refused. Why he refused is a mystery. On
the one side it is said that the assault of the
fortified French lines took on a new value after
the costly "victory" of Malplaquet; on the
other that Marlborough was "oppressed by the
hostility of the Queen and the growing power of
his foes in England." Yet had he not written
that he was seeking a battle that would be his
last? The truth is that once again the General
was in a thoroughly defeatist mood. A fortnight
later, on June 14/25, Sunderland, his son-in-law
and ever the Queen's *bête-noire*, was dismissed
from the Cabinet and replaced as Secretary of
State by a "moderate." Marlborough had
vainly appealed to Shrewsbury to save Sunderland. The divided Whig Government failed to
make any exertion on Sunderland's behalf and
on the contrary wrote jointly to Marlborough
asking him not to show his resentment and to
retain his command. Marlborough agreed, but
henceforward washed his hands even of foreign
politics. After the fall of Douai, Villars again
gave Marlborough the chance to fight another
Malplaquet, but he refused and turned aside to
besiege a number of minor fortresses. His mind

seems to have been paralysed by the political
disasters at home.

Although he and Eugene commanded 120,000
men, they failed to achieve anything of substantial military importance and thereby abandoned
the last chance of forcing Louis XIV to sue for
peace on the abject terms of which they both
approved.

While Marlborough was being reduced to stalemate in Flanders, Godolphin was being steadily
outmanœuvred in London.   Slowly but surely
Queen Anne, acting on Harley's advice, under-
mined the Whigs.   The proud Junto of 1708
crumpled before a series of oblique attacks and
up went the cry of " *Sauve qui peut !* "   The Duke
of Somerset and the Earl of Halifax were detached
from their Cabinet colleagues ; to the Duke of
Newcastle, another "moderate," Harley held
out the promise of a reconstructed coalition
Ministry similar to that of 1702.   On August 7
Queen Anne struck her boldest blow : she dismissed without a kind word her Lord Treasurer
Godolphin who had served his country with
single-minded devotion for eight years.   But still
the leading Whigs clung to their offices, incapable
of perceiving the rising storm.   Even Harley
himself did not appreciate how strong the Tory
reaction of the electorate would be.   But Shrewsbury saw the one big issue when he told the
Austrian Ambassador that "England is badly
in need of peace."   When in the autumn the
General Election took place, Anne showed that
she had correctly interpreted the trend of

feeling in the country. The Whigs were beaten by a majority of three to one ; there could thus be no question of a moderate or middle Ministry ; Harley came back as the head of a purely Tory administration pledged to make peace.

Marlborough deeply resented the treatment of Godolphin. But he found it impossible to give up his command in the middle of the campaign and Godolphin himself begged him not to do so. But Godolphin's curt dismissal finally ensured that no striking military results would be obtained that year. On July 31/August 11, just before Godolphin went, Marlborough wrote to him :

> I am of opinion that after the siege of Aire I shall have it in my power to attack Calais . . . but I see so much malice levelled at me, that I am afraid it is not safe for me to make any proposition ; fearing, if it should not suc-ceed, my enemies might turn it to my dis-advantage.

He had to suffer a series of humiliations at the hands of Harley's new Ministry. Cardonel, his former secretary, was deprived of his office of Secretary at War ; Cadogan, his right-hand man, ceased to be envoy to the Dutch ; a commission was set up in London to decide Army promo-tions ; and three of his subordinates were cashiered for having drunk the toast " damna-tion and confusion to the new Ministry." Fearful of the General's popularity, the new Ministers hired pamphleteers to ridicule his avarice and condemn his ambition. But in spite of these insults and his inability to win a major military

success, Marlborough remained abroad until the
end of the year, seeing to the conquest of a group
of fortresses on the north-eastern frontier of
France – Bethune, Aire and St. Venant – which
prepared the way for a good campaign in the
following year. Whatever criticisms may be
made of his retention of offices after his return to
England, his patriotic conduct under the grossest
provocation after Godolphin's dismissal cannot
be questioned.

Marlborough delayed as long as possible his
return to England and his interview with the
" new vipers "– as he called them – who now
governed the country. But when he did come
early in January, 1711, he was pleased and surprised at the warm welcome which he received
from the public. Abroad the armies and the
Allies had rallied to him on the defeat of his
political friends. The Dutch had cried, " Lord !
what will become of us ? " should he relinquish
his command. He was in fact the symbol of the
continuing unity of the Grand Alliance, and
without him the new Tory Ministers began to
be afraid that they could not exact reasonable
peace terms from the French. So Harley now
decided to abandon his intention of forcing Marlborough from his offices, but Queen Anne,
always bolder than Harley, insisted for her part
that Sarah must be dismissed from Court. Consequently Marlborough's first task on his return
was to try to induce the Queen not to affront
him through his wife. Sarah had been trying to
blackmail the Queen by threatening the publication

of Anne's letters to her. Marlborough would have none of that. But he submitted to every indignity to try to save his wife's position. He grovelled before the Queen. He carried to her a humble letter from Sarah which asserted that he could not live six months if she were sacked. The Queen was unmoved and demanded Sarah's gold key of office as Groom of the Stole within two days. Sarah returned the key at once, but before she went she exacted a cash payment of £18,000 which she claimed the Queen owed her, and took care to remove even the brass locks from the doors of her Palace apartments. On other questions Anne was equally stiff with her General. Marlborough was told that there could be no question of reinstating his three favourite officers who had been cashiered and that he must not suffer any votes of thanks to him to be moved in Parliament. He was also advised that " he must draw a line between all that has passed and all that is to come and that he must begin entirely upon a new foot." A combination of threats and promises was used to prevent his resignation.

Marlborough has left one record of his own reasons for keeping his command under such humiliating conditions. He told a Hanoverian Minister that he did not want to expose himself to the censure of those foreigners who were his friends for refusing to serve the Alliance and that he wished to remain in a position to ensure the Protestant succession to the British Throne. But this, of course, is what he had to tell the Hanoverian Court which held the Protestant

successor. As usual, there was a mixture of
patriotic and personal motives in his mind.
Blenheim Palace, that " monstrous pile " on
which he had set his heart, was still but half
completed and the Tory Treasury had stopped
payments. A promise was given him that the
payments would be resumed if he kept his command. Hence he went quickly back to the war
in March, while unbeknown to him the British
Ministry was setting on foot secret negotiations
for a separate peace with France.

These secret negotiations were made easier by
an unexpected event. In April the young
Emperor Joseph I died and his brother, the
Archduke Charles, the Allies' candidate for the
Spanish Throne and Empire, succeeded to the
vast Habsburg dominions. Charles was at the
time in Catalonia, which was the only part of
Spain retained by the Allies after ten years of
war. His succession to the throne of Vienna
enabled the Tory Government to argue that the
balance of power in Europe would be upset if a
Habsburg ruler held sway not only over the whole
of Austria and Hungary, the bulk of Italy and
modern Belgium, but Spain and the Indies as
well, and that therefore the Whig view that peace
should not be made without Spain being torn
from Philip of Anjou was no longer valid. The
Emperor's death also had a disastrous effect
upon the military campaign in France. Eugene,
who had joined Marlborough at Douai, had to
return to Germany with most of his troops to
ensure that Charles was elected Holy Roman
Emperor in his brother's stead, and Villars, the

French commander, by detaching a few of his troops to the Rhine, was able to draw off from France a higher proportion of the Allied troops.

The situation at the beginning of the 1711 campaign was that a breach had been blown in the last defences of France. In consequence of the previous campaign, Arras and Cambrai remained the last important fortresses of the French frontier barrier between Ypres on the north-east and Valenciennes, Maubeuge and Le Quesnoy farther south. Villars had done his best to protect the most vulnerable area with field fortifications, nicknamed the Ne Plus Ultra lines, stretching through Arras to beyond Bouchain, a small but useful fortress south-west of Valenciennes. In spite of his temporary conciliation with Harley, Marlborough was ill and depressed after the departure of Eugene. But at length he pulled himself together and determined to penetrate the Ne Plus Ultra lines. These were covered to the east by a number of rivers and inundations and were naturally weakest at their western end. Villars therefore concentrated his forces to the west, where Marlborough sat opposite him in the plains of Lens. Marlborough now planned an ingenious stratagem. One of the causeways across the rivers to the east of the Ne Plus Ultra was guarded by a fort named Arleux. By taking this fort, strengthening its defences and then allowing Villars to recapture it, Marlborough induced Villars himself to demolish it. Then Marlborough circulated the story that he was going to attack Villars' whole

Im

army at the other end of the lines. But while
feinting to the west he detached Cadogan to
collect an advance guard from Douai and also
sent his artillery to the east. At nightfall on
August 5, after feinting again to the French left,
Marlborough rapidly marched with the whole of
his army to the right of the long French lines.
He thus gained several hours on the French
which they could not hope to overtake. He
crossed the River Sensée at two points near the
demolished fort of Arleux and was over the Ne
Plus Ultra lines without firing a shot. The
French were not far behind, however, and a day
later were drawn up in a strong position to the
south-west of the Allied forces. Villars had his
wings well covered and it was out of the question
for Marlborough to attack him so long as he
dreaded a second Malplaquet. Marlborough
was censured in Holland for not attacking the
enemy and had to explain that

> there is not one general or other officer that
> have the least judgment in these matters but
> must allow it was altogether impossible to
> attack the enemy with any probable hope of
> success.

Instead, he laid siege to Bouchain. This siege
was unique in the annals of eighteenth-century warfare. Villars was compelled to watch Marlborough
bombard the town into surrender, although he
had an army larger by some 6,000 men than
that of the Allies. Marlborough constructed an
elaborate series of earthworks to protect his communications, while he had the usual lines of

circumvallation to the south to cut off the garrison from the French army. While Marlborough bombarded Bouchain, Villars bombarded Marlborough's siege army. But by September 12 the siege was successful at the cost of some 4,000 casualties and the garrison obliged to surrender as prisoners of war.

This proved to be Marlborough's last military achievement. He tried to persuade the Home Government to support him in the siege of Le Quesnoy and to allow his men to winter in the field in preparation for an early start in 1712, instead of going into their usual winter quarters. But Harley and St. John were now, virtually unknown to Marlborough, deeply committed in the peace negotiations. They withheld supplies and sent Marlborough a " bamboozling " letter. On this minor key ended Marlborough's splendid military career. The Duke was personally proud of the 1711 campaign and had more tapestries (which now hang in Blenheim Palace) made in commemoration of it than of any other campaign. He had finally refuted the silly but popular story that he could do nothing without Prince Eugene and had penetrated the strong French defensive lines and taken an important fortress in the teeth of a superior French army commanded by the best French general.

Nevertheless, Marlborough's military record would have been even finer if it had ended in 1708 and peace had been concluded in 1709. For since 1708, although the French frontier was crossed and the last raw French army in the field, the Allies, with their veteran soldiers and victorious general, had achieved comparatively little. It is hard to believe that even if he had been in command in 1712 the French would ever again have been reduced to the straits in which they were after the battle of Oudenarde and the fall of Lille. But everywhere there was war weariness. The limit of endurance had been reached. So long as the French could be made to promise trading concessions in the Spanish Empire and Belgium went to a weak naval power, there was no convincing British case for continuing the war until Spain, never an easy country to subdue, had been reconquered. When Marlborough asserted that without the unheard-of step of wintering in the field there was no guarantee of a successful campaign in the next year, he was in effect confessing that the war had reached stalemate. Queen Anne wrote bluntly that " the Duke of Marlborough shows plainer than ever by this new project his unwillingness for peace." And it may be that she was right ; that the war waged for a now almost hopeless end had become so much part and parcel of his life that he could not conceive of life without it.

CHAPTER XIII

WINTER SUNSHINE: 1711–1722

Tory peace negotiations – Marlborough's opposition and dismissal – charges of peculation – Treaty of Utrecht, 1713 – Marlborough in exile – return – last days.

WHILE Marlborough was waging his last campaign, the British Government was secretly completing its peace negotiations with France. In April, 1711, a series of new proposals which were particularly generous in regard to openings for British trade in the Spanish Empire were forwarded to London from Versailles. The Dutch were to be guaranteed a substantial fortress barrier and were informed of these proposals. The inner British Cabinet was convinced that they offered a sufficient basis for negotiations, and Queen Anne personally authorized Matthew Prior, the poet, to go to Versailles and pursue the matter in secret there. The Tories were ready for a partition of the Spanish inheritance, as provided in William III's Partition Treaties and the Grand Alliance signed by Marlborough in 1701 (see pp. 34–35). The negotiations soon took a favourable turn. Prior's mission could not be concealed and Marlborough learned of it, but only indirectly. Indeed, it was not until September, after the discussions had been transferred back to London, that Harley, now Earl of Oxford and Lord Treasurer, at last wrote and informed

the Duke, nominally his Cabinet colleague, that
the French had made an offer of a general peace
" by the canal of England " and – this was the
crux – that the Queen had said " she would
enter into no separate treaty." But in fact a
separate treaty in the form of three preliminary
agreements was signed between Britain and
France on September 27/October 8 whereby
the British demands were fully met but the
Allied claims were only specified in general
terms, no care being taken to fulfil the promises
of the Anglo-Dutch Barrier Treaty of 1709 or to
secure Spain for the Emperor. Marlborough
was kept in the dark about these transactions,
but suspected and disliked their general character.
Sarah Marlborough, delightedly poking her
finger into the pie again, employed pamphleteers
to attack the Government, while the Duke himself, whose relations with the Court of Hanover
were close and amicable, incited Anne's destined
successor, the Dowager Electress of Hanover, to
protest against abandoning Spain to the French
claimant. Marlborough significantly came home
from the war accompanied by a Hanoverian
Ambassador sent to protest formally against the
Anglo-French agreement.

The day after his return, November 19, Marlborough saw the Queen and spoke against the
Ministerial moves and showed himself, in Anne's
own words, " dejected and uneasy." But, as
always, he was burning his boats slowly, willing
upon an appropriate inducement to put out
the fire. When Parliament opened the Queen
announced that a time and a place had been

settled for the peace conference (it was to meet at Utrecht in January). A fierce debate followed in the House of Lords and Marlborough had to define his position. Supported by the Whig majority in that House, he spoke firmly if not vehemently against " peace without Spain " and indignantly denied that he was trying to prolong the war for his own personal ends.

The Government was defeated in the Lords by eight votes, but was, of course, upheld by the Tory majority in the Commons. In these circumstances the Queen had no alternative but to dismiss Marlborough from her service. There was nothing improper about her decision. Marlborough was a member of the Cabinet and not merely a soldier under orders. Although the doctrine of joint Cabinet responsibility was in its infancy, it was impossible to keep in office so influential a statesman who was openly opposed to the peace proposals on which the Queen's Government had decided. But the method of Marlborough's dismissal was shabby. A trumped-up charge of peculation in his capacity of Commander-in-Chief was brought against him by a partisan Parliamentary Committee. He was accused of wrongfully accepting a percentage on the Army bread contracts and on the pay of foreign mercenaries. The charge was ridiculous. He was fully authorized, both by the Queen and by the Government of 1702 and by the foreign princes concerned, to take the percentage to spend on his excellent intelligence service ; and the deduction from the bread contracts was a recognized perquisite which he employed for the same

purpose. His immediate successor as Commander-in-Chief was not only offered but took
both percentages. The Tory rulers merely tried to
cover the late general with mud in the hope that
some of it would stick so as to offset the force of
his criticism of their peace plans. Queen Anne dismissed him with a letter so brutally ungrateful that
he threw it in the fire. He was abruptly relieved
of his offices on the last day of 1711. The next
day the Duke of Ormonde was made Commander-
in-Chief in his place and twelve peers were created
to break the hostile majority in the Lords.

Marlborough retained his friends amongst the
Whigs and his popularity, especially in the Army,
and he remained a potentially dangerous Opposition leader, but on the whole he held his hand.
His famous colleague, Prince Eugene, arrived in
London – too late as usual – and vainly tried to
stop the progress of the British peace negotiations.
But he associated himself publicly with Marlborough and bestowed praise upon him sufficient
to stop the mouths of those who would have
lauded his prowess at Marlborough's expense.
When Eugene returned to the war he found that
Marlborough's successor, Ormonde, had been
ordered by St. John not to fight a battle while
the negotiations were in progress, to the bitter
humiliation of Marlborough's veterans. Marlborough later took part in a debate on these
notorious " restraining orders " and inquired
pertinently how Ormonde could be expected to
undertake a siege without running the risk of a
battle. Deserted entirely by the British troops,
Eugene could not prevent the Dutch being

defeated at the battle of Denain on July 24, 1712, and the French were thus assured of obtaining better terms than they had offered at Gertruydenberg two years earlier, a result which reflected not only on the " restraining orders " but on Marlborough's and his friends' inability to conclude peace earlier.

Marlborough withdrew to his country house at Holywell, near St. Albans. He could not live at Blenheim Palace, which was still only half built, for the Ministry, while threatening to sue him for his " illegal " perquisites, stopped paying the wòrkmen. The Duke and Duchess lived together quietly although not undisturbed by calumny. Marlborough used his influence to help needy disabled officers, wrote to Vienna about his princedom of Mindelheim and took care of his sick friend Godolphin. In August a clergyman who dined at St. Albans saw the Duke and Duchess and " heard his Grace reprimand the Duchess for sitting at prayers but she obeyed not." After the death of Godolphin in September, Marlborough, alarmed at growing threats of lawsuits and even prosecution, decided to go abroad. Queen Anne was glad enough to grant him a passport, and there is even a story that Harley blackmailed him into going abroad by threatening to publish one of his secret letters to the Jacobites which had come into his hands. There was certainly a secret meeting between them. But, as Mr. Churchill writes, if this story is true Harley was " forcing an open door with a battering ram." On November 24 the Duke shook the dust of an ungrateful England from his feet.

During Marlborough's absence the group of
separate agreements between France and the
Allies (excluding the Emperor) known collectively
as the Treaty of Utrecht were at last signed (April
11, 1713). Philip of Anjou was recognized as
Philip V of Spain and the Indies, but both France
and Spain promised that the two Bourbon Crowns
should never be united. Great Britain obtained
Hudson's Bay, Newfoundland, Nova Scotia,
Acadia, St. Christopher, Minorca and Gibraltar,
as well as trading privileges in South America
and a monopoly of the slave export trade. The
Dutch, for their part, gained a considerable
barrier of fortresses (but less than had been
promised them), certain forts guarding the mouth
of the Scheldt and shared the trade of Belgium
with Britain. The Duke of Savoy obtained
Sicily ; the Elector of Bavaria was restored to his
dominions conquered by Marlborough in 1704.
In consequence of the war and the Treaty,
Holland was soon to cease to be an effective
commercial rival to Britain, who also became
the supreme naval power and laid her Empire
on firm foundations. The Whig merchants and
financiers who had supported the war so vigor-
ously did well out of the Tory peace.

Marlborough criticized the general character of
the Treaty on two grounds. First, he said it was a
betrayal of the Allies. (The Emperor was so disgusted that he went on with the war.) Secondly,
Marlborough objected to Spain being ruled by a
Bourbon prince in spite of his renunciation of his
right of succession to the French Crown. To
Marlborough it could be, and was, answered that

the Dutch had contemplated a separate agreement
with France and the Emperor had actually concluded separate agreements with France in 1707,
and that this was the only assured way of making
peace. Moreover, both the Allies gained hand-
somely from the partition of the Spanish Empire.
As to the question of Spain and the Bourbons, why
had he changed his mind since 1701 ? In any case,
he overestimated the ease with which that country
could be conquered. As in other political questions, undoubtedly personal factors influenced his
view of the Treaty. For instance, he had long
hoped that after the peace the Emperor would
fulfil his promise of making him Governor-
General of the Spanish Netherlands and that the
Dutch would at last approve. If the Allies were
alienated by the peace treaties they would not
trouble to gratify the British general who had
won the war for them. There was also the princedom of Mindelheim in conquered Bavaria to be
considered. Some of the very few letters which
the Duke wrote in exile concerned this principality, which he visited in June, 1713 ; in the
long run he lost this too, and although he complained to Eugene, was not compensated. However, Marlborough neither wrote nor uttered any
criticisms of the Treaty when in exile. Some say
that the resumption of the payments on the
building of Blenheim Palace was the price paid
for his silence.

When he first went abroad, although welcomed
by magistrates and common people in Belgium
and Holland, the Duke was lonely. He even had
no secretary and was forced to pen letters in his

own hand throughout. But in due course he was joined by his wife and his friend Cadogan. For over six months he stayed in Frankfort, leading a not wholly lazy existence. Thence he entered into communication with the Courts of both Hanover and St. Germains, where dwelt the rivals for the British succession. He begged the Old Pretender for a pardon, but whereas he sent kind words to " James III," he actually entered into elaborate arrangements with the Electress of Hanover and her son, the future George I, as to the military and constitutional steps to be taken on Anne's death. And although he sent Mary of Modena, mother of the Pretender, a small sum, he offered to lend £10,000 to the future George I. Where his treasure lay, there was his heart also. When they heard at the beginning of 1714 that the Queen had been taken ill, the Marlboroughs, both mightily homesick after a year of exile, prepared to return. But the Queen recovered, so they waited until the Parliament, which had been elected in 1713, rose in July. On July 30, 1714, Marlborough was already waiting to embark, and while he was on the high seas the Queen expired (August 1) just after she had again dismissed a former favourite, the serpentine Harley, and, half-unconscious, handed his White Staff to the Whig potentate, the Duke of Shrewsbury, in the interests of the Protestant succession.

The accession of the German-speaking George I of Hanover to the throne of Great Britain was peacefully accomplished with scarcely a groan from the impotent Jacobites. Marlborough, enthusiastically welcomed in London, was at once restored to the post of Commander-in-Chief and Master-General of the Ordnance, and a Whig Government, including his son-in-law Sunderland, replaced the divided and nerveless Tories. In due course Marlborough had his revenge on the Tory Ministers, St. John, Viscount Bolingbroke and Harley, Earl of Oxford, who had been responsible for his dismissal in 1711. He frightened St. John from the country with threats of an Act of Attainder and one of his last public appearances was to vote (in vain) for Harley's impeachment in 1717. As Commander-in-Chief, the Duke reinstated his old officers in the commands from which they had been expelled by the Tories and championed the claims of the foreign Protestant officers who had served him so well in Flanders. He also exerted his influence with Eugene to find positions for officers barred from the British service by religious and other disabilities. So there was a little fitful sunshine in the winter of his life.

But Marlborough had small influence with the new rulers of his country. They were not ungrateful for his services. Yet the Whigs never entirely trusted him ; nor did the new King. And though he carried on, out of habit may be, his polite intercourse with St. Germains, he was past successful intrigue or active warfare. He directed only from his armchair the operations which were to bring about the defeat of the Scottish Jacobite rising of 1715 – his last snub to the exiles he had bamboozled so long.

The Duke, now sixty-four, dwelt quietly at

Marlborough House, built by the Duchess on
Wren's designs in 1709–11, at Windsor Lodge and
at Holywell, St. Albans. He did not live to see
the completion of Blenheim Palace (finished in
1727), by which he set such passionate store. The
mighty dynast had no son. Of his four daughters,
Elizabeth Bridgewater, the third, predeceased him
in March, 1714, and his favourite, Anne Sunderland, died in April, 1716. The second death was
probably a cause of his first paralytic seizure in
May of that year. A second seizure followed in
August. He made a partial recovery and spent
time taking the waters at Tunbridge Wells and
Bath. He used, so it was said, to walk to the Spa
at Bath so as to save the sixpence on the chairman.
He was, as he knew, but the shadow of the handsome soldier who had won the battle of Oudenarde at the age of fifty-eight. One day he gazed
at his portrait by Kneller and murmured, " This
was once a man." His domestic peace was constantly rent. Sarah, still in full possession of her
explosive faculties, " prowled round his couch like
a she-bear guarding her slowly dying mate and
tearing all, friend or foe, who approached"
(Churchill). She quarrelled alike with his friend
and successor as Commander-in-Chief, General
Cadogan, with Sir John Vanbrugh, the architect
of Blenheim, and with her two surviving daughters,
Henrietta Godolphin and Mary Montagu. Marlborough's last extant letter, written in 1721, says :
" I believe I am the worse to see my children
live so ill with a mother for whom I must have the
greatest tenderness and regard." He died, rich
and admired, on June 16, 1722, at the age of

seventy-two and was buried in Westminster
Abbey. His body was later removed to Blenheim
Palace. There is the monument to the greatest,
if not the noblest or most selfless, of British soldiers.

BIBLIOGRAPHY

Apart from Mr. Winston Churchill's *Marlborough : his Life and Times* (4 vols., 1933–8) the principal sources for Marlborough's own correspondence are Archdeacon W. Coxe, *Memoirs of the Duke of Marlborough* (3 vols., 1818–9), the letters in which are partly but not entirely reprinted by Churchill, and Sir George Murray, *Letters and Dispatches* (5 vols., 1845). Lord Wolseley (*The Life of John Churchill to the Accession of Queen Anne*, 2 vols., 1894) and Dr. Stuart Reid (*John and Sarah, Duke and Duchess of Marlborough*, 1914), also had access to the Blenheim papers. Their works have been superseded, but still contain a little important material. A few valuable Marlborough letters are in Sarah's *Private Correspondence* (2 vols., carelessly edited, 1838) and the *Bath Papers* (Historical MSS. Commission, Vol. I). Dr. Roderick Geikie also had access to the Blenheim papers for his posthumously published researches on the Dutch Barrier Treaty (Geikie and Montgomery, *The Dutch Barrier, 1705–1719*, 1930) which throw a flood of light on Marlborough as a diplomatist. Werner Reese, *Das Ringen um Frieden und Sicherheit 1708–1709* (1933), contains some new materials and views.

Professor G. M. Trevelyan, *England under Queen Anne* (3 vols.), gives an admirable background for the heroic period, and Mr. David Ogg, *England in the Reign of Charles II*, for the earlier period. Mr. Keith Feiling's *History of the Tory Party, 1640–1714*, is essential for an understanding of party politics. Excellent books on Marlborough's military career are C. T. Atkinson, *Marlborough* (1921), and Frank Taylor, *Wars of Marlborough* (2 vols., 1921). Marlborough's attitude to sea power is described in J. H. Owen, *War at Sea under Queen Anne, 1702–8* (1938). The best of Sarah Marlborough's lives is by Kathleen Campbell (1932). There are detailed Marlborough bibliographies in Churchill.